The Phoenix by Thomas Middleton

Thomas Middleton was born in London in April 1580 and baptised on 18th April.

Middleton was aged only five when his father died. His mother remarried but this unfortunately fell apart into a fifteen year legal dispute regarding the inheritance due Thomas and his younger sister.

By the time he left Oxford, at the turn of the Century, Middleton had and published Microcynicon: Six Snarling Satirese which was denounced by the Archbishop of Canterbury and publicly burned.

In the early years of the 17th century, Middleton wrote topical pamphlets. One – Penniless Parliament of Threadbare Poets was reprinted several times and the subject of a parliamentary inquiry.

These early years writing plays continued to attract controversy. His writing partnership with Thomas Dekker brought him into conflict with Ben Jonson and George Chapman in the so-called War of the Theatres.

His finest work with Dekker was undoubtedly The Roaring Girl, a biography of the notorious Mary Frith.

In the 1610s, Middleton began another playwriting partnership, this time with the actor William Rowley, producing another slew of plays including Wit at Several Weapons and A Fair Quarrel.

The ever adaptable Middleton seemed at ease working with others or by himself. His solo writing credits include the comic masterpiece, A Chaste Maid in Cheapside, in 1613.

In 1620 he was officially appointed as chronologer of the City of London, a post he held until his death.

The 1620s saw the production of his and Rowley's tragedy, and continual favourite, The Changeling, and of several other tragicomedies.

However in 1624, he reached a peak of notoriety when his dramatic allegory A Game at Chess was staged by the King's Men. Though Middleton's approach was strongly patriotic, the Privy Council silenced the play after only nine performances at the Globe theatre, having received a complaint from the Spanish ambassador.

What happened next is a mystery. It is the last play recorded as having being written by Middleton.

Thomas Middleton died at his home at Newington Butts in Southwark in the summer of 1627, and was buried on July 4th, in St Mary's churchyard which today survives as a public park in Elephant and Castle.

Index of Contents

Dramatis Personae
The DUKE of Ferrara
INFESTO, a lord
LUSSURIOSO, a lord
PRODITOR, a lord
NOBLES
Prince PHOENIX, the Duke's son
FIDELIO, his servant
NIECE to FALSO
THREE SOLDIERS of the sea
The CAPTAIN, Castiza's husband
CASTIZA, Fidelio's mother
The GROOM of an inn
SUITORS to TANGLE
TANGLE, a lawyer
The JEWELLER'S WIFE, Falso's daughter
Her BOY
The KNIGHT
His LACKEY
SUITORS to FALSO
FALSO, a justice
LATRONELLO, his servant
FURTIVO, his servant
TWO GENTLEMEN, friends of Falso's brother
SERVANT to PRODITOR

FUCATO, Falso's servant
CONSTABLE and OFFICERS
QUIETO, a reformed lawyer
Quieto's BOY
MAID to the JEWELLER'S WIFE
GENTLEMAN, a reveller
A DRAWER

ACT I

SCENE I – A Chamber in the Palace of the Duke of Ferrara

Enter the old **DUKE** of Ferrara, nobles, **PRODITOR, LUSSURIOSO**, and **INFESTO**, with **ATTENDANTS**.

DUKE
My lords,
Know that we, far from any natural pride,
Or touch of temporal sway, have seen our face
In our grave council's foreheads, where doth stand
Our truest glass, made by time's wrinkled hand.
We know we're old; my days proclaim me so.
Forty-five years I've gently ruled this dukedom;
Pray heaven it be no fault,
For there's as much disease, though not to th' eye,
In too much pity as in tyranny.

INFESTO
Your grace hath spoke it right.

DUKE
I know that life
Has not long course in me; 'twill not be long
Before I show that kings have mortal bodies
As well as subjects. Therefore, to my comfort,
And your successful hopes, I have a son
Whom I dare boast of—

LUSSURIOSO
Whom we all do boast of;
A prince elder in virtues than in years.

INFESTO
His judgment is a father to his youth.

PRODITOR [Aside]
Ay, ay, would he were from court!

INFESTO
Our largest hopes grow in him.

PRODITOR
And 'tis the greatest pity, noble lord,
He is untraveled.

LUSSURIOSO
'Tis Indeed, my lord.

PRODITOR
Had he but travel to his time and virtue—
[Aside] Oh, he should ne'er return again!

DUKE
It shall be so: what is in hope begun
Experience quickens; travel confirms the man,
Who else lives doubtful, and his days oft sorry;
Who's rich in knowledge has the stock of glory.

PRODITOR
Most true, my royal lord.

DUKE
Someone attend our son.

[Enter Prince **PHOENIX**, attended by **FIDELIO**

INFESTO
See, here he comes, my lord.

DUKE
Oh, you come well.

PHOENIX
'Tis always my desire, my worthy father.

DUKE
Your serious studies, and those fruitful hours
That grow up into judgment, well become
Your birth, and all our loves; I weep that you are my son,
But virtuously I weep, the more my gladness.
We have thought good and meet by the consent
Of these our nobles, to move you toward travel,
The better to approve you to yourself,
And give your apter power foundation:
To see affections actually presented,

E'en by those men that owe them, yields more profit,
Ay, more content, than singly to read of them,
Since love or fear make writers partial.
The good and free example which you find
In other countries, match it with your own,
The ill to shame the ill, which will in time
Fully instruct you how to set in frame
A kingdom all in pieces.

PHOENIX
Honour'd father,
With care and duty I have listened to you.
What you desire, in me it is obedience:
I do obey in all, knowing for right,
Experience is a kingdom's better sight.

PRODITOR
Oh, 'tis the very luster of a prince.
Travel! 'Tis sweet and generous.

DUKE
He that knows how to obey, knows how to reign;
And that true knowledge have we found in you.
Make choice of your attendants.

PHOENIX
They're soon chose;
Only this man, my lord, a loving servant of mine.

DUKE
What, none but he?

PHOENIX
I do entreat no more;
For that's the benefit a private gentleman
Enjoys beyond our state, when he notes all,
Himself unnoted.
For, should I bear the fashion of a prince,
I should then win more flattery than profit;
And I should give 'em time and warning then
To hide their actions from me: if I appear a sun,
They'll run into the shade with their ill deeds,
And so prevent me.

PRODITOR [Aside]
A little too wise, a little too wise to live long.

DUKE

You have answered us with wisdom: let it be.
Things private are best known through privacy.

[Exeunt. Manet **PHOENIX** and **FIDELIO**.

PHOENIX
Stay you, my elected servant.

FIDELIO
My kind lord.

PHOENIX
The **DUKE** my father has a heavy burden
Of years upon him.

FIDELIO
My lord, it seems so, for they make him stoop.

PHOENIX
Without dissemblance he is deep in age;
He bows unto his grave. I wonder much
Which of his wild nobility it should be—
For none of his sad council has a voice in't—
Should so far travel into his consent
To set me over into other kingdoms
Upon the stroke and minute of his death?

FIDELIO
My lord, 'tis easier to suspect them all,
Than truly to name one.

PHOENIX
Since it is thus,
By absence I'll obey the Duke my father
And yet not wrong myself.

FIDELIO
Therein, my lord,
You might be happy twice.

PHOENIX
So it shall be;
I'll stay at home and travel.

FIDELIO
Would your grace
Could make that good!

PHOENIX

I can. And indeed a prince need not travel farther than his own kingdom, if he apply himself faithfully, worthy the glory of himself and expectation of others. And it would appear far nobler industry in him to reform those fashions that are already in his country than to bring new ones in which have neither true form nor fashion; to make his court an owl, city an ape, and the country a wolf preying upon the ridiculous pride of either. And therefore I hold it a safer stern upon this lucky advantage, since my father is near his setting, and I upon the eastern hill to take my rise, to look into the heart and bowels of this dukedom, and in disguise mark all abuses ready for reformation or punishment.

FIDELIO

Give me but leave unfeignedly to admire you,
Your wisdom is so spacious and so honest.

PHOENIX

So much have the complaints and suits of men seven, nay, seventeen years neglected, still interposed by coin and great enemies, prevailed with my pity that I cannot otherwise think but there are infectious dealings to most offices, and foul mysteries throughout all professions. And therefore I nothing doubt but to find travel enough within myself, and experience, I fear, too much. Nor will I be curious to fit my body to the humblest form and bearing, so the labour may be fruitful: for how can abuses that keep low come to the right view of a prince unless his looks lie level with them, which else will be longest hid from him, he shall be the last man sees 'em.
For oft between king's eyes and subjects' crimes
Stands there a bar of bribes; the under office
Flatters him next above it, he the next,
And so of most, or many.
Every abuse will choose a brother:
'Tis through the world, this hand will rub the other.

FIDELIO

You have set down the world briefly, my lord.

PHOENIX

But how am I assur'd of faith in thee?
Yet I durst trust thee.

FIDELIO

Let my soul be lost
When it shall loose your secrets. Nor will I
Only be a preserver of them, but,
If you so please, an assister.

PHOENIX

It suffices.
That king stands sur'st who by his virtues rises
More than by birth or blood; that prince is rare
Who strives in youth to save his age from care.
Let's be prepar'd. Away!

FIDELIO
I'll follow your grace.

[Exit **PHOENIX.**

Thou wonder of all princes, president, and glory,
True Phoenix, made of an unusual strain!
Who labours to reform is fit to reign.
How can that king be safe that studies not
The profit of his people? See where comes
The best part of my heart, my love.

[Enter **NIECE.**

NIECE
Sir, I am bound to find you; I heard newly
Of sudden travel which his grace intends,
And only but yourself to accompany him.

FIDELIO
You heard in that little beside the truth;
Yet not so sudden as to want those manners
To leave you unregarded.

NIECE
I did not think so unfashionably of you.
How long is your return?

FIDELIO
'Tis not yet come to me, scarce to my lord,
Unless the Duke refer it to his pleasure;
But long I think it is not: the duke's age,
If not his apt experience, will forbid it.

NIECE
His grace commands, I must not think amiss.
Farewell.

FIDELIO
Nay, stay, and take this comfort:
You shall hear often from us, I'll direct
Where you shall surely know; and I desire you
Write me the truth, how my new father-in-law
The Captain bears himself toward my mother;
For that marriage knew nothing of my mind,
It never flourish'd in any part of my affection.

NIECE

Methinks she's much disgrac'd herself.

FIDELIO
Nothing so,
If he be good, and will abide the touch;
A Captain may marry a lady, if he can sail
Into her good will.

NIECE
Indeed, that's all.

FIDELIO
'Tis all
In all. Commend me to thy breast; farewell.

[Exit **NIECE**.

So by my lord's firm policy we may see,
To present view, what absent forms would be.

[Exit.

SCENE II – A Room in the Captain's House

Enter the **CAPTAIN** with soldiering **FELLOWS**.

FIRST SOLDIER
There's noble purchase, Captain!

SECOND SOLDIER
Nay, admirable purchase.

THIRD SOLDIER
Enough to make us proud forever.

CAPTAIN
Hah?

FIRST SOLDIER
Never was opportunity so gallant.

CAPTAIN
Why, you make me mad!

SECOND SOLDIER
Three ships, not a poop less.

THIRD SOLDIER
And every one so wealthily burdened, upon my manhood.

CAPTAIN
Pox on't, and now am I tied e'en as the devil would ha't.

FIRST SOLDIER
CAPTAIN, of all men living, I would ha' sworn thou would'st ne'er have married.

CAPTAIN
'Sfoot, so would I myself, man. Give me my due; you know I ha' sworn all heaven over and over?

FIRST SOLDIER
That you have, i'faith.

CAPTAIN
Why, go to, then.

FIRST SOLDIER
Of a man that has tasted salt water to commit such a fresh trick!

CAPTAIN
Why, 'tis abominable, I grant you, now I see't!

FIRST SOLDIER
Had there been fewer women—

SECOND SOLDIER
And among those women fewer drabs—

THIRD SOLDIER
And among those drabs fewer pleasing—

CAPTAIN
Then 't 'ad been something.

FIRST SOLDIER
But when there are more women, more common, pretty sweethearts, than ever any age could boast of—

CAPTAIN
And I to play the artificer and marry: to have my wife dance at home, and my ship at sea, and both take in salt water together! Oh, lieutenant, thou'rt happy, thou keep'st a wench.

FIRST SOLDIER
I hope I am happier than so, Captain, for o' my troth, she keeps me.

CAPTAIN
How? Is there any such fortunate man breathing? And I so miserable to live honest! I envy thee, lieutenant, I envy thee, that thou art such a happy knave. Here's my hand among you, share it equally: I'll to sea with you.

SECOND SOLDIER
There spoke a noble Captain!

CAPTAIN
Let's hear from you; there will be news shortly.

FIRST SOLDIER
Doubt it not, Captain.

[Exeunt all but **CAPTAIN**.

CAPTAIN
What lustful passion came aboard of me that I should marry; was I drunk? Yet that cannot altogether hold, for it was four o'clock i' th' morning; had it been five, I would ha' sworn it. That a man is in danger every minute to be cast away, without he have an extraordinary pilot that can perform more than a man can do! And to say truth, too, when I'm abroad, what can I do at home? No man living can reach so far. And what a horrible thing 'twould be to have horns brought me at sea, to look as if the devil were i' th' ship! And all the great tempests would be thought of my raising: to be the general curse of all merchants! And yet they likely are as deep in as myself, and that's a comfort. Oh, that a Captain should live to be married! Nay, I that have been such a gallant salt-thief should yet live to be married. What a fortunate elder brother is he, whose father being a rammish plowman, himself a perfumed gentleman spending the labouring reek from his father's nostrils in tobacco, the sweat of his father's body in monthly physic for his pretty, queasy harlot. He sows apace, i' th' country; the tailor o'ertakes him i' th' city, so that oftentimes before the corn comes to earing, 'tis up to the ears in high collars, and so at every harvest the reapers take pains for the mercers: ha! why this is stirring happiness indeed. Would my father had held a plow so, and fed upon squeez'd curds and onions, that I might have bath'd in sensuality! But he was too ruttish himself to let me thrive under him, consumed me before he got me, and that makes me so wretched now to be shackled with a wife, and not greatly rich, neither.

[Enter his lady, **CASTIZA**.

CASTIZA
Captain, my husband.

CAPTAIN
'Slife, call me husband again and I'll play the Captain and beat you.

CASTIZA
What has disturb'd you, sir, that you now look
So like an enemy upon me?

CAPTAIN
Go make a widower, hang thyself!

CASTIZA
How comes it that you are so opposite
To love and kindness? I deserve more respect,
But that you please to be forgetful of it.
For love to you did I neglect my state,
Chide better fortunes from me,
Gave the world talk, laid all my friends at waste.

CAPTAIN
The more fool you. Could you like none but me?
Could none but I supply you? I am sure
You were sued by far worthier men,
Deeper in wealth and gentry.
What could'st thou see in me, to make thee dote
So on me? If I know I am a villain,
What a torment's this! Why didst thou marry me?
You think, as most of your insatiate widows,
That captains can do wonders, when 'las,
The name does often prove the better man.

CASTIZA
That which you urge should rather give me cause
To repent than yourself.

CAPTAIN
Then to that end
I do't.

CASTIZA
What a miserable state
Am I led into!

[Enter **SERVANT**.

CAPTAIN
How now, sir?

SERVANT
Count Proditor
Is now alighted.

CAPTAIN
What, my lord? I must
Make much of him, he'll one day write me cuckold;
'Tis good to make much of such a man:
E'en to my face he plies it hard. I thank him.

[Enter **PRODITOR**.

What, my worthy lord?

PRODITOR
I'll come to you
In order, Captain.

[Kisses **CASTIZA**.

CAPTAIN [Aside]
Oh, that's in order!
A kiss is the gamut to pricksong.

PRODITOR
Let me salute you, Captain.

[Exit **CASTIZA**.

CAPTAIN
My dear
Esteemed count, I have a life for you.

PRODITOR
Hear you the news?

CAPTAIN
What may it be, my lord?

PRODITOR
My lord, the duke's son, is upon his travel
To several kingdoms.

CAPTAIN
May it be possible, my lord,
And yet so little rumour'd?

PRODITOR
Take't of my truth;
Nay, 'twas well manag'd, things are as they are handl'd:
But all my care is still, pray heaven he return
Safe, without danger, Captain.

CAPTAIN
Why, is there
Any doubt to be had of that, my lord?

PRODITOR

Ay, by my faith, Captain:
Princes have private enemies, and great.
Put case a man should grudge him for his virtues,
Or envy him for his wisdom; why, you know,
This makes him lie barebreasted to his foe.

CAPTAIN
That's full of certainty, my lord; but who
Be his attendants?

PRODITOR
Thence, CAPTAIN, comes the fear;
But singly attended, neither--[Aside] my best gladness—
Only by your son-in-law, Fidelio.

CAPTAIN
Is it to be believ'd? I promise you, my lord, then I begin to fear him myself; that fellow will undo him. I durst undertake to corrupt him with twelvepence over and above, and that's a small matter; h'as a whorish conscience; he's an inseparable knave, and I could ne'er speak well of that fellow.

PRODITOR
All we of the younger house, I can tell you, do doubt him much. The lady's remov'd: shall we have your sweet society, Captain?

CAPTAIN
Though it be in mine own house, I desire
I may follow your lordship.

PRODITOR
I love to avoid strife;
[Aside] Not many months Phoenix shall keep his life.

[Exit.

CAPTAIN
So, his way is in; he knows it.
We must not be uncourteous to a lord;
Warn him our house, 'twere vild. His presence is
An honour. If he lie with our wives, 'tis for
Our credit; we shall be the better trusted:
'Tis a sign we shall live i' th' world. Oh, tempests and whirlwinds! Who but that man whom the forefinger cannot daunt, that makes his shame his living, who but that man, I say, could endure to be throughly married? Nothing but a divorce can relieve me: any way to be rid of her would rid my torment. If all means fall, I'll kill or poison her and purge my fault at sea. But first I'll make gentle try of a divorce: but how shall I accuse her subtle honesty? I'll attach this lord's coming to her, take hold of that, ask counsel: and now I remember, I have acquaintance with an old, crafty client, who, by the puzzle of suits and shifting of courts, has more tricks and starting-holes than the dizzy pates of fifteen attorneys; one that has been muzzled in law like a bear, and led by the ring of his spectacles from office to office:

Him I'll seek out with haste; all paths I'll tread,
All deaths I'll die, ere I die married.

[Exit.

SCENE III – Another Room in the Captain's House

Enter **PRODITOR** with **CASTIZA**.

PRODITOR
Puh, you do resist me hardly.

CASTIZA
I beseech your lordship, cease in this; 'tis never to be granted. If you come as a friend unto my honour and my husband, you shall be ever welcome; if not, I must entreat it—

PRODITOR
Why, assure yourself, madam, 'tis not the fashion.

CASTIZA
'Tis more my grief, my lord; such as myself
Are judg'd the worse for such.

PRODITOR
Faith, you're too nice:
You'll see me kindly forth?

CASTIZA
And honourably welcome.

[Exeunt.

SCENE IV – A Room in an Inn

Enter a **GROOM** before **PHOENIX** and **FIDELIO**, alighting into an inn.

GROOM
Gentlemen, you're most neatly welcome.

PHOENIX
You're very cleanly, sir; prithee, have a care to our geldings.

GROOM
Your geldings shall be well considered.

FIDELIO
Considered?

PHOENIX
Sirrah, what guests does this inn hold now?

GROOM
Some five and twenty gentlemen, besides their beasts.

PHOENIX
Their beasts?

GROOM
Their wenches, I mean, sir; for your worship knows that those that are under men are beasts.

PHOENIX
How does your mother, sir?

GROOM
Very well in health, I thank you heartily, sir.

PHOENIX
And so is my mare, i'faith.

GROOM
I'll do her commendations indeed, sir.

FIDELIO
Well kept up, shuttlecock!

PHOENIX
But what old fellow was he that newly alighted before us?

GROOM
Who, he? As arrant a crafty fellow as e'er made water on horseback: some say he's as good as a lawyer; marry, I'm sure he's as bad as a knave. If you have any suits in law, he's the fittest man for your company; he's been so towed and lugg'd himself that he is able to afford you more knavish counsel for ten groats than another for ten shillings.

PHOENIX
A fine fellow! But do you know him to be a knave, and will lodge him?

GROOM
Your worship begins to talk idly; your bed shall be made presently: if we should not lodge knaves, I wonder how we should be able to live honestly. Are there honest men enough, think you, in a term-time to fill all the inns in the town? And, as far as I can see, a knave's gelding eats no more hay than an honest man's; nay, a thief's gelding eats less, I'll stand to't, his master allows him a better ordinary. Yet I have

my eightpence, day and night. 'Twere more for our profit, I wus, you were all thieves, if you were so contented. I shall be called for: give your worships good morrow.

[Exit.

PHOENIX
A royal knave, i'faith. We have happened into a godly inn.

FIDELIO
Assure you, my lord, they belong all to one church.

PHOENIX
This should be some old, busy, turbulent fellow: villainous law-worn, that eats holes into poor men's causes.

[Enter **TANGLE** with two **SUITORS**, and **GROOM**.

FIRST SUITOR
May it please your worship to give me leave?

TANGLE
I give you leave, sir: you have your veniam. Now fill me a brown toast, sirrah.

GROOM
Will you have no drink to't, sir?

TANGLE
Is that a question in law?

GROOM
Yes, in the lowest court, i' th' cellar, sir.

TANGLE
Let me ha't remov'd presently, sir.

GROOM
It shall be done, sir.

[Exit.

TANGLE
Now as you were saying, sir. I'll come to you immediately, too.

PHOENIX
Oh, very well, sir.

TANGLE
I'm a little busy, sir.

FIRST SUITOR
But as how, sir?

TANGLE
I pray, sir?

FIRST SUITOR
He's brought me into the court; marry, my adversary has not declared it.

TANGLE
Non declaravit adversarius, sayst thou? What a villain's that! I have a trick to do thee good: I will get thee out a proxy, and make him declare, with a pox to him.

FIRST SUITOR
That will make him declare, to his sore grief; I thank your good worship. But put case he do declare?

TANGLE
Si declarasset, if he should declare there—

FIRST SUITOR
I would be loath to stand out to the judgment of that court.

TANGLE
Non ad judicium? Do you fear corruption? Then I'll relieve you again. You shall get a supersedeas non molestandum, and remove it higher.

FIRST SUITOR
Very good.

TANGLE
Now if it should ever come to a testificandum, what be his witnesses?

FIRST SUITOR
I little fear his witnesses.

TANGLE
Non metuis testes? More valiant man than Orestes!

FIRST SUITOR [Giving him money]
Please you, sir, to dissolve this into wine, ale, or beer. I come a hundred mile to you, I protest, and leave all other counsel behind me.

TANGLE
Nay, you shall always find me a sound card; I stood not a' th' pillory for nothing in eighty-eight, all the world knows that. Now let me dispatch you, sir: I come to you, presenter.

SECOND SUITOR

Faith, the party hath remov'd both body and cause with a habeas corpus.

TANGLE
Has he that knavery? But has he put in bail above, canst tell?

SECOND SUITOR
That, I can assure your worship, he has not.

TANGLE
Why, then, thy best course shall be to lay out more money, take out a procedendo, and bring down the cause and him with a vengeance.

SECOND SUITOR
Then he will come indeed.

TANGLE
As for the other party, let the audita querela alone; take me out a special supplicavit, which will cost you enough, and then you pepper him. For the first party, after the procedendo you'll get costs; the cause being found, you'll have a judgment; nunc pro tunc, you'll get a venire facias to warn your jury, a decem tales to fill up the number, and a capias utlagatem for your execution.

SECOND SUITOR
I thank you, my learned counsel.

PHOENIX [To **FIDELIO**]
What a busy caterpillar's this! Let's accost him in that manner.

FIDELIO
Content, my lord.

PHOENIX
Oh, my old admirable fellow, how have I all this while thirsted to salute thee! I knew thee in octavo of the Duke—

TANGLE
In octavo of the Duke? I remember the year well.

PHOENIX
By th' mass, a lusty, proper man!

TANGLE
Oh, was I?

PHOENIX
But still in law.

TANGLE

Still in law? I had not breath'd else now; 'tis very marrow, very manna to me to be in law: I'd been dead ere this else. I have found such sweet pleasure in the vexation of others that I could wish my years over and over again, to see that fellow a beggar, that bawling knave a gentleman, a matter brought e'en to a judgment today, as far as e'er 'twas to begin again tomorrow. Oh, raptures! Here a writ of demur, there a procedendo, here a sursurrara, there a capiendo, tricks, delays, money-laws!

PHOENIX
Is it possible, old lad?

TANGLE
I have been a term-trotter myself any time this five and forty years: a goodly time and a gracious: in which space I ha' been at least sixteen times beggar'd, and got up again; and in the mire again, that I have stunk again, and yet got up again.

PHOENIX
And so clean and handsome now?

TANGLE
You see it apparently; I cannot hide it from you. Nay, more, in felici hora be it spoken, you see i' me old, yet have I at this present nine and twenty suits in law.

PHOENIX
Deliver us, man!

TANGLE
And all not worth forty shillings.

PHOENIX
May it be believ'd?

TANGLE
The pleasure of a man is all.

PHOENIX
An old fellow, and such a stinger!

TANGLE
A stake pull'd out of my hedge, there's one; I was well beaten, I remember, that's two; I took one abed with my wife again her will, that's three; I was call'd cuckold for my labor, that's four; I took another bed again, that's five; then one called me wittol, that's six; he kill'd my dog for barking, seven; my maidservant was knock'd at that time, eight; my wife miscarried with a push, nine; and sic de ceteris. I have so vex'd and beggar'd the whole parish with process, subpoenas, and suchlike molestations, they are not able to spare so much ready money from a term as would set up a new weathercock; the churchwardens are fain to go to law with the poor's money.

PHOENIX [Aside]
Fie, fie!

TANGLE

And I so fetch up all the men every term-time, that 'tis impossible to be at civil cuckoldry within ourselves, unless the whole country rise upon our wives.

FIDELIO

O'my faith, a pretty policy!

PHOENIX

Nay, an excellent stratagem. But of all, I most wonder at the continual substance of thy wit, that, having had so many suits in law from time to time, thou has still money to relieve 'em.

FIDELIO

He's the best fortune for that; I never knew him without.

TANGLE

Why do you so much wonder at that? Why, this is my course: my mare and I come up some five days before a term.

PHOENIX

A good decorum.

TANGLE

Here I lodge, as you see, amongst inns and places of most receipt—

PHOENIX

Very wittily.

TANGLE

By which advantage I dive into countrymen's causes; furnish 'em with knavish counsel, little to their profit; buzzing into their ears this course, that writ, this office, that ultimum refugium—as you know, I have words enow for the purpose.

PHOENIX

Enow i' conscience, i'faith.

TANGLE

Enow i' law, no matter for conscience. For which busy and laborious sweating courtesy they cannot choose but feed me with money, by which I maintain mine own suits. Ho, ho, ho!

PHOENIX

Why, let me hug thee; caper in mine arms.

TANGLE

Another special trick I have, nobody must know it, which is to prefer most of those men to one attorney whom I affect best, to answer which kindness of mine he will sweat the better in my cause and do them the less good; take't of my word, I help'd my attorney to more clients the last term than he will dispatch all his lifetime: I did it!

PHOENIX
What a noble, memorable deed was there!

[Enter **GROOM**.

GROOM
Sir.

TANGLE
Now, sir?

GROOM
There's a kind of Captain very robustiously inquires for you.

TANGLE
For me? A man of war? A man of law is fit for a man of war: we have no leisure to say prayers; we both kill o' Sunday mornings. [To **PHOENIX**] I'll not be long from your sweet company.

PHOENIX
Oh, no, I beseech you.

[Exit **TANGLE** with **GROOM**.

FIDELIO
What Captain might this be?

PHOENIX
Thou angel sent amongst us, sober Law,
Made with meek eyes, persuading action,
No loud, immodest tongue,
Voic'd like a virgin, and as chaste from sale,
Save only to be heard, but not to rail;
How has abuse deform'd thee to all eyes,
That where thy virtues sat, thy vices rise?
Yet why so rashly, for one villain's fault,
Do I arraign whole man? Admired Law,
Thy upper parts must need be sacred, pure,
And incorruptible; they're grave and wise:
'Tis but the dross beneath 'em, and the clouds
That get between thy glory and their praise,
That make the visible and foul eclipse;
For those that are near to thee are upright,
As noble in their conscience as their birth;
Know that damnation is in every bribe,
And rarely put it from 'em; rate the presenters,
And scourge 'em with five years' imprisonment,
For offering but to tempt 'em.
This is true justice exercis'd and us'd:

Woe to the giver when the bribe's refus'd!
'Tis not their will to have law worse than war,
Where still the poor'st die first;
To send a man without a sheet to his grave,
Or bury him in his papers.
'Tis not their mind it should be, nor to have
A suit hang longer than a man in chains,
Let him be ne'er so fasten'd. They least know
That are above the tedious steps below:
I thank my time, I do.

FIDELIO
I long to know what Captain this should be.

PHOENIX
See where the bane of every cause returns.

[Enter **TANGLE**, with **CAPTAIN**.

FIDELIO
'Sfoot, 'tis the Captain, my father-in-law, my lord!

PHOENIX
Take heed.

CAPTAIN
The divorce shall rest then, and the five hundred crowns shall stand in full force and virtue.

TANGLE
Then do you wisely, Captain.

CAPTAIN
Away sail I; fare thee well.

TANGLE
A lusty crack of wind go with thee.

CAPTAIN
But ah!—

TANGLE
Hah?

CAPTAIN
Remember, a scrivener.

TANGLE
I'll have him for thee.

[Exit **CAPTAIN**.

Why, thus am I sought after by all professions. Here's a weatherbeaten Captain, who, not long since new married to a lady widow, would now fain have sued a divorce between her and him, but that her honesty is his only hindrance: to be rid of which, he does determine to turn her into white money; and there's a lord, his chapman, has bid five hundred crowns for her already.

FIDELIO
How?

TANGLE
Or for his part, or whole, in her.

PHOENIX
Why, does he mean to sell his wife?

TANGLE
His wife? Ay, by th' mass, he would sell his soul if he knew what merchant would lay out money upon't; and some of 'em have need of one, they swear so fast.

PHOENIX
Why, I never heard of the like.

TANGLE
Non audivisti, didst ne'er hear of that trick? Why, Pistor, a baker, sold his wife t'other day to a cheesemonger, that made cake and cheese; nother to a cofferer; a third to a common player: why, you see 'tis common. Ne'er fear the CAPTAIN; he has not so much wit to be a precedent himself. I promis'd to furnish him with an odd scrivener of mine own, to draw the bargain and sale of his lady. Your horses stored here, gentlemen?

PHOENIX
Ay, ay, ay.

TANGLE
I shall be busily plung'd till towards bedtime above the chin in profundis.

[Exit.

PHOENIX
What monstrous days are these!
Not only to be vicious most men study,
But in it to be ugly; strive to exceed
Each other in the most deformed deed.

FIDELIO
Was this her private choice? Did she neglect
The presence and opinion of her friends

For this?

PHOENIX
I wonder who that one should be,
Should so disgrace that reverend name of lord
So loathsomely to buy adultery?

FIDELIO
We may make means to know.

PHOENIX
Take courage, man; we'll beget some defense.

FIDELIO
I am bound by nature.

PHOENIX
I by conscience.
To sell his lady! Indeed, she was a beast
To marry him, and so he makes of her.
Come, I'm thorough now I'm entered.

[Exeunt.

SCENE V – A Street in Ferrara

Enter **JEWELLER'S WIFE** with a **BOY**.

JEWELLER'S WIFE
Is my sweet Knight coming? Are you certain he's coming?

BOY
Certain, forsooth; I am sure I saw him out of the barber's shop window ere I would come away.

JEWELLER'S WIFE
A barber's shop? Oh, he's a trim Knight! Would he venture his body into a barber's shop, when he knows 'tis as dangerous as a piece of Ireland? Oh, yonder, yonder, he comes! Get you back again, and look you say as I advis'd you.

[Enter **KNIGHT** with **LACKEY**.

BOY
You know me, mistress!

JEWELLER'S WIFE
My mask, my mask!

[Exit **BOY**.]

KNIGHT
My sweet Revenue!

JEWELLER'S WIFE
My Pleasure, welcome! I have got single; none but you shall accompany me to the justice of peace, my father's.

KNIGHT
Why, is thy father justice of peace, and I not know it?

JEWELLER'S WIFE
My father? I'faith, sir, ay; simply though I stand here a citizen's wife, I am a justice of peace's daughter.

KNIGHT
I love thee the better for thy birth.

JEWELLER'S WIFE
Is that your lackey yonder, in the steaks of velvet?

KNIGHT
He's at thy service, my sweet Revenue, for thy money paid for 'em.

JEWELLER'S WIFE
Why, then, let him run a little before, I beseech thee, for o'my troth, he will discover us else.

KNIGHT
He shall obey thee: before, sirrah, trudge.

[Exit **LACKEY**.

But do you mean to lie at your father's all night?

JEWELLER'S WIFE
Why should I desire your company else?

KNIGHT
'Sfoot, where shall I lie, then?

JEWELLER'S WIFE
What an idle question's that? Why, do you think I cannot make room for you in my father's house as well as in my husband's? They're both good for nothing else.

KNIGHT
A man so resolute in valour as a woman in desire were an absolute leader!

[Exeunt.

Scene VI – A Room in Falso's House

Enter two Suitors with the justice, **FALSO**.

FIRST SUITOR
May it please your good worship, master justice—

FALSO
Please me and please yourself; that's my word.

FIRST SUITOR
The party your worship sent for will by no means be brought to appear.

FALSO
He will not? Then what would you advise me to do therein?

FIRST SUITOR
Only to grant your worship's warrant, which is of sufficient force to compel him.

FALSO
No, by my faith! You shall not have me in that trap: am I sworn justice of peace, and shall I give my warrant to fetch a man against his will? Why, there the peace is broken. We must do all quietly; if he come he's welcome, and, as far as I can see yet, he's a fool to be absent; ay, by this gold is he--[Aside] which he gave me this morning.

FIRST SUITOR
Why, but may it please your good worship—

FALSO
I say again, please me and please yourself; that's my word still.

FIRST SUITOR
Sir, the world esteems it a common favour, upon the contempt of the party, the justice to grant his warrant.

FALSO
Ay, 'tis so common, 'tis the worse again; 'twere the better for me 'twere otherwise.

FIRST SUITOR
I protest, sir, and this gentleman can say as much, it lies upon my half undoing.

FALSO
I cannot see yet that it should be so; I see not a cross yet.

FIRST SUITOR

I beseech your worship show me your immediate favour, and accept this small trifle but as a remembrance to my succeeding thankfulness.

FALSO

Angels? I'll not meddle with them; you give 'em to my wife, not to me.

FIRST SUITOR

Ay, ay, sir.

FALSO

But, I pray, tell me now, did the party viva voce, with his own mouth, deliver that contempt, that he would not appear, or did you but jest in't?

FIRST SUITOR

Jest? No, o' my troth, sir, such was his insolent answer.

FALSO

And do you think it stood with my credit to put up such an abuse? Will he not appear, says he? I'll make him appear with a vengeance. Latronello!

[Enter **LATRONELLO**.

LATRONELLO

Does your worship call?

FALSO

Draw me a strong-limb'd warrant for the gentleman speedily; he will be bountiful to thee. Go and thank him within.

FIRST SUITOR

I shall know your worship hereafter.

[Exeunt **SUITORS** and **LATRONELLO**].

FALSO

Ay, ay, prithee do. Two angels one party, four another: and I think it a great spark of wisdom and policy, if a man come to me for justice, first to know his griefs by his fees, which be light and which be heavy; he may counterfeit else, and make me do justice for nothing. I like not that, for when I mean to be just, let me be paid well for't: the deed so rare purges the bribe.

[Enter **FURTIVO**.

How now, what's the news, thou art come so hastily? How fares my knightly brother?

FURTIVO

Troth, he ne'er fared worse in his life, sir; he ne'er had less stomach to his meat since I knew him.

FALSO
Why, sir?

FURTIVO
Indeed, he's dead, sir.

FALSO
How, sir?

FURTIVO
Newly deceas'd, I can assure your worship: the tobacco-pipe new dropp'd out of his mouth before I took horse, a shrewd sign; I knew then there was no way but one with him. The poor pipe was the last man he took leave of in this world, who fell in three pieces before him and seem'd to mourn inwardly, for it look'd as black i' th' mouth as my master.

FALSO
Would he die so like a politician, and not once write his mind to me?

FURTIVO
No, I'll say that for him, sir; he died in the perfect state of memory, made your worship his full and whole executor, bequeathing his daughter and with her all his wealth only to your disposition.

FALSO
Did he make such a godly end, sayest thou? Did he die so comfortably, and bequeath all to me?

FURTIVO
Your Niece is at hand, sir, the will, and the witnesses.

FALSO
What a precious joy and comfort's this, that a justice's brother can die so well, nay, in such a good and happy memory, to make me full executor. Well, he was too honest to live, and that made him die so soon. Now, I beshrew my heart, I am glad he's in heaven; he's left all his cares and troubles with me, and that great vexation of telling of money: yet I hope he had so much grace to turn his white money into gold, a great ease to his executor.

FURTIVO
See, here comes your Niece, my young mistress, sir.

[Enter **NIECE** and **TWO GENTLEMEN**.

FALSO
Ah, my sweet Niece, let me kiss thee and drop a tear between thy lips! One tear from an old man is a great matter; the cooks of age are dry. Thou hast lost a virtuous father, to gain a notable uncle.

NIECE
My hopes now rest in you next under heaven.

FALSO

Let 'em rest, let 'em rest.

FIRST GENTLEMAN
Sir—

FALSO
You're most welcome ere ye begin, sir.

FIRST GENTLEMAN
We are both led by oath and dreadful promise
Made to the dying man at his last sense,
First to deliver these into your hands,
The sureties and revealers of his state—

FALSO
Good.

FIRST GENTLEMAN
With this his only daughter and your Niece,
Whose fortunes are at your disposing set;
Uncle and father are in you both met.

FALSO
Good, i'faith, a wellspoken gentleman; you're not an esquire, sir?

FIRST GENTLEMAN
Not, sir.

FALSO
Not, sir? More's the pity; by my faith, better men than you are, but a great many worse: you see I have been a scholar in my time, though I'm a justice now. Niece, you're most happily welcome; the charge of you is wholly and solely mine own: and since you are so fortunately come, Niece, I'll rest a perpetual widower.

NIECE
I take the meaning chaster than the words;
Yet I hope well of both, since it is thus,
His phrase offends least that's known humourous.

FALSO [Reading the will]
I make my brother," says he, "full and whole executor": honestly done of him, i'faith! Seldom can a man get such a brother. And here again, says he, very virtuously, "I bequeath all to him and his disposing": an excellent fellow, o' my troth, would you might all die no worse, gentlemen!

[Enter **KNIGHT** with **JEWELLER'S WIFE**.

FIRST GENTLEMAN
But as much better as might be.

KNIGHT
Bless your uprightness, master justice!

FALSO
You're most soberly welcome, sir. Daughter, you've that ye kneel for; rise, salute your weeping cousin.

JEWELLER'S WIFE
Weeping, cousin? [They speak apart.]

KNIGHT [Aside]
Eye to weeping is very proper, and so is the party that spake it, believe me, a pretty, fine, slender, straight, delicate-knit body.
Oh, how it moves a pleasure through our senses!
How small are women's waists to their expenses!
I cannot see her face, that's under water yet.

JEWELLER'S WIFE
News as cold to the heart as an old man's kindness: my uncle dead!

NIECE
I have lost the dearest father!

FALSO [Reading the will]
"If she marry by your consent, choice and liking, make her dowry five thousand crowns"--[Aside] hum, five thousand crowns? Therefore by my consent she shall ne'er marry; I will neither choose for her, like of it, nor consent to't.

KNIGHT [Aside]
Now, by the pleasure of my blood, a pretty cousin! I would not care if I were as near kin to her as I have been to her kinswoman.

FALSO
Daughter, what gentleman might this be?

JEWELLER'S WIFE
No gentleman, sir, he's a Knight.

FALSO
Is he but a KNIGHT? Troth, I would a' sworn he'd been a gentleman, to see, to see, to see.

JEWELLER'S WIFE
He's my husband's own brother, I can tell you, sir.

FALSO
Thy husband's brother? Speak certainly, prithee.

JEWELLER'S WIFE

I can assure you, father, my husband and he have lain both in one belly.

FALSO
I'll swear then he is his brother indeed, and by the surer side. I crave hearty pardon, sweet kinsman, that thou hast stood so long unsaluted in the way of kindred.
Welcome to my board; I have a bed for thee.
My daughter's husband's brother shall command
Keys of my chests and chambers.
I have stable for thy horse, chamber for thyself,
And a loft above for thy lousy lackey:
All sit, away with handkerchers, dry up eyes;
At funeral we must cry; now let's be wise.

[Exeunt all but **KNIGHT** and **JEWELLER'S WIFE**.

JEWELLER'S WIFE
I told you his affection.

KNIGHT
It falls sweetly.

JEWELLER'S WIFE
But here I bar you from all plots tonight;
The time is yet too heavy to be light.

KNIGHT
Why, I'm content; I'll sleep as chaste as you,
And wager night by night who keeps most true.

JEWELLER'S WIFE
Well, we shall see your temper.

[Exeunt.

ACT II

SCENE I — A Room in the Inn

Enter **PHOENIX** and **FIDELIO**.

PHOENIX
Fear not me, Fidelio; become you that invisible rope-maker, the scrivener, that binds a man as he walks, yet all his joints at liberty, as well as I'll fit that common folly of gentry, the easy-affecting venturer, and no doubt our purpose will arrive most happily.

FIDELIO

Chaste duty, my lord, works powerfully in me; and rather than the poor lady my mother should fall upon the common side of rumour to beggar her name, I would not only undergo all habits, offices, disguis'd professions, though e'en opposite to the temper my blood holds, but, in the stainless quarrel of her reputation, alter my shape forever.

PHOENIX
I love thee wealthier, thou hast a noble touch; and by this means, which is the only safe means to preserve thy mother from such an ugly land- and sea-monster as a counterfeit Captain is, he resigning and basely selling all his estate, title, right, and interest in his lady, as the form of the writing shall testify, What otherwise can follow but to have
A lady safe deliver'd of a knave?

FIDELIO
I am in debt my life to the free goodness of your inventions.

PHOENIX
Oh, they must ever strive to be so good!
Who sells his vow is stamped the slave of blood.

[Exeunt.

SCENE II – A Room in the Captain's House

Enter **CAPTAIN**, his lady **CASTIZA** following him.

CAPTAIN
Away!

CASTIZA
CAPTAIN, my husband—

CAPTAIN
Hence! We're at a price for thee, at a price,
Wants but the telling and the sealing; then—

CASTIZA
Have you no sense, neither of my good name
Or your own credit?

CAPTAIN
Credit? Pox of credit
That makes me owe so much! It had been
Better for me by a thousand royals
I had lost my credit seven year ago.
'T'as undone me: that's it that makes me fly:
What need I to sea else, in the springtime,

When woods have leaves, to look upon bald oak?
Happier that man, say I, whom no man trusts!
It makes him valiant, dares outface the prisons,
Upon whose carcass no gown'd raven jets:
Oh, he that has no credit owes no debts!
'Tis time I were rid on't.

CASTIZA
Oh, why do you
So willfully cherish your own poison,
And breathe against the best of life, chaste credit?
Well may I call it chaste, for, like a maid,
Once falsely broke, it ever lives decay'd.
Oh, Captain, husband, you name that dishonest
By whose good power all that are honest live;
What madness is it to speak ill of that
Which makes all men speak well! Take away credit,
By which men amongst men are well reputed,
That man may live, but still lives executed.
Oh, then, show pity to that noble title,
Which else you do usurp. You're no true Captain
To let your enemies lead you; foul disdain
And everlasting scandal, oh, believe it!
The money you receive for my good name
Will not be half enough to pay your shame.

CAPTAIN
No?
I'll sell thee then to the smock. See, here comes
My honourable chapman.

[Enter **PRODITOR** and his **SERVANT**.

CASTIZA
Oh, my poison!
Him whom mine honour and mine eye abhors.

[Exit.

PRODITOR
Lady! What, so unjovially departed?

CAPTAIN [Aside]
Fine she-policy! She makes my back her bolster, but before my face she not endures him. Tricks!

PRODITOR
Captain, how haps it she remov'd so strangely?

CAPTAIN
Oh, for modesty's cause awhile, my lord;
She must restrain herself, she's not yours yet.
Beside, it were not wisdom to appear
Easy before my sight.
Fah! Wherefore serves modesty but to pleasure a lady now and then, and help her from suspect? That's the best use 'tis put to.

PRODITOR
Well observ'd of a Captain!

CAPTAIN
No doubt you'll be soon friends, my lord.

PRODITOR
I think no less.

CAPTAIN
And make what haste I can to my ship, I durst wager you'll be under sail before me.

PRODITOR
A pleasant voyage, Captain!

CAPTAIN
Ay, a very pleasant voyage as can be. I see the hour is ripe: here comes the prison's bawd, the bond-maker, one that binds heirs before they are begot.

PRODITOR
And here are the crowns, Captain. [To **SERVANT**] Go, attend!
Let our bay courser wait.

Enter **PHOENIX** and **FIDELIO**, both disguised.

SERVANT
It shall be obey'd.

[Exit **SERVANT**.

CAPTAIN [Aside to **FIDELIO**]
A farmer's son, is't true?

FIDELIO [Aside to **CAPTAIN**]
He's crowns to scatter!

CAPTAIN
I give you your salute, sir.

PHOENIX

I take it not unthankfully, sir.

CAPTAIN
I hear a good report of you, sir: you've money.

PHOENIX
I have so, true.

CAPTAIN
An excellent virtue.

PHOENIX [Aside]
Ay, to keep from you. [To **CAPTAIN**] Hear you me, Captain? I have a certain generous itch, sir, to lose a few angels in the way of profit: 'tis but a game at tennis,
Where, if the ship keep above line, 'tis three to one;
If not, there's but three hundred angels gone.

CAPTAIN
Is your venture three hundred? You're very preciously welcome; here's a voyage toward will make us all—

PHOENIX [Aside]
Beggarly fools and swarming knaves!

PRODITOR [Aside to **CAPTAIN**]
Captain, what's he?

CAPTAIN [Aside to **PRODITOR**]
Fear him not, my lord, he's a gull, he ventures with me; some filthy farmer's son: the father's a Jew and the son a gentleman. Fa!

PRODITOR [Aside to **CAPTAIN**]
Yet he should be a Jew, too, for he is new come from giving over swine.

CAPTAIN [Aside to **PRODITOR**]
Why, that in our country makes him a gentleman.

PRODITOR
Go to! Tell your money, Captain.

CAPTAIN
Read aloft, scrivener.

[Counting the money]

One, two—

FIDELIO [Reads]

"To all good and honest Christian people, to whom this present writing shall come: know you for a certain, that I, Captain, for and in the consideration the sum of five hundred crowns, have clearly bargained, sold, given, granted, assigned, and set over, and by these presents do clearly bargain, sell, give, grant, assign, and set over, all the right, estate, title, interest, demand, possession, and term of years to come, which I the said Captain have, or ought to have"—

PHOENIX [Aside]
If I were as good as I should be.

FIDELIO
"In and to Madonna Castiza, my most virtuous, modest, loving, and obedient wife"—

CAPTAIN
By my troth, my lord, and so she is—three, four, five, six, seven—

PHOENIX [Aside]
The more slave he that says it, and not sees it.

FIDELIO
"Together with all and singular those admirable qualities with which her noble breast is furnished."

CAPTAIN
Well said, scrivener, hast put 'em all in? You shall hear now, my lord.

FIDELIO
"In primis, the beauties of her mind, chastity, temperance, and above all, patience"—

CAPTAIN
You have bought a jewel, i'faith, my lord—nine and thirty, forty—

FIDELIO
"Excellent in the best of music, in voice delicious, in conference wise and pleasing, of age contentful, neither too young to be apish, nor too old to be sottish"—

CAPTAIN
You have bought as lovely a pennyworth, my lord, as e'er you bought in your life.

PRODITOR
Why should I buy her else, Captain?

FIDELIO
"And, which is the best of a wife, a most comfortable, sweet companion"—

CAPTAIN
I could not afford her so, i'faith, but that I am going to sea, and have need of money.

FIDELIO
"A most comfortable, sweet companion"—

PRODITOR
What, again? The scrivener reads in passion.

FIDELIO
I read as the words move me; yet if that be a fault, it shall be seen no more: "which said Madonna Castiza lying, and yet being in the occupation of the said Captain"—

CAPTAIN
Nineteen. Occupation? Pox on't, out with "occupation," a Captain is of no occupation, man.

PHOENIX [Aside]
Nor thou of no religion.

FIDELIO
Now I come to the habendum: "to have and to hold, use and"—

CAPTAIN
Use? Put out "use," too, for shame, till we are all gone, I prithee.

FIDELIO
"And to be acquitted of and from all former bargains, former sales"—

CAPTAIN
Former sales?—nine and twenty, thirty—by my troth, my lord, this is the first time that ever I sold her.

PRODITOR
Yet the writing must run so, Captain.

CAPTAIN
Let it run on, then—nine and forty, fifty—

FIDELIO
"Former sales, gifts, grants, surrenders, re-entries"—

CAPTAIN
For re-entries, I will not swear for her.

FIDELIO
"And furthermore, I the said, of and for the consideration of the sum of five hundred crowns to set me aboard, before these presents, utterly disclaim forever any title, estate, right, interest, demand, or possession, in or to the said Madonna Castiza, my late virtuous and unfortunate wife"—

PHOENIX [Aside]
Unfortunate indeed! That was well plac'd.

FIDELIO

"As also neither to touch, attempt, molest, or encumber any part or parts whatsoever, either to be named or not to be named, either hidden or unhidden, either those that boldly look abroad, or those that dare not show their faces"—

CAPTAIN
Faces? I know what you mean by faces: scrivener, there's a great figure in faces.

FIDELIO
"In witness whereof, I the said Captain have interchangeably set to my hand and seal, in presence of all these, the day and date above written."

CAPTAIN
Very good, sir, I'll be ready for you presently—four hundred and twenty, one, two, three, four, five—

PHOENIX [Aside]
Of all deeds yet, this strikes the deepest wound
Into my apprehension.
Reverend and honourable matrimony,
Mother of lawful sweets, unshamed mornings,
Dangerless pleasures, thou that mak'st the bed
Both pleasant and legitimately fruitful:
Without thee,
All the whole world were soiled bastardy.
Thou are the only and the greatest form
That put'st a difference between our desires
And the disordered appetites of beasts,
Making their mates those that stand next their lusts.
Then, with what base injury is thy goodness paid!
First, rare to have a bride commence a maid,
But does beguile joy of the purity,
And is made strict by power of drugs and art,
An artificial maid, a doctor'd virgin,
And so deceives the glory of his bed;
A foul contempt against the spotless power
Of sacred wedlock. But if chaste and honest,
There is another devil haunts marriage,
None fondly loves but knows it: jealousy,
That wedlock's yellow sickness,
That whispering separation every minute,
And thus the curse takes his effect or progress.
The most of men in their first sudden furies
Rail at the narrow bounds of marriage,
And call't a prison; then it is most just
That the disease o' th' prison, jealousy,
Should still affect 'em. But oh! Here I am fix'd
To make sale of a wife, monstrous and foul,
An act abhorr'd in nature, cold in soul.
Who that has man in him could so resign

To make his shame the poesy to the coin?

CAPTAIN
Right, i'faith, my lord; fully five hundred.

PRODITOR
I said how you should find it, Captain; and with this competent sum you rest amply contented?

CAPTAIN
Amply contented.

FIDELIO
Here's the pen, Captain: your name to the sale.

CAPTAIN
'Sfoot, dost take me to be a penman? I protest I could ne'er write more than A B C, those three letters, in my life.

FIDELIO
Why, those will serve, Captain.

CAPTAIN
I could ne'er get further.

PHOENIX
Would you have got further than A B C? [Aside] Ah, Base Captain: that's far enough, i'faith.

FIDELIO
Take the seal off, Captain.

CAPTAIN
It goes on hardly and comes off easily.

PHOENIX
Ay, just like a coward.

FIDELIO
Will you write witness, gentleman?

CAPTAIN
He? He shall; prithee come and set thy hand for witness, rogue. Thou shall venture with me?

PHOENIX
Nay, then I ha' reason, Captain, that commands me.

[Writes.]

CAPTAIN [Aside]

What a fair fist the pretty whoreson writes, as if he had had manners and bringing up: a farmer's son! His father damns himself to sell musty corn, while he ventures the money; 'twill prosper well at sea, no doubt. He shall ne'er see't again.

FIDELIO
So, Captain, you deliver this as your deed?

CAPTAIN
As my deed; what else, sir?

PHOENIX [Aside]
The ugliest deed that e'er mine eye did witness.

CAPTAIN
So, my lord, you have her; clip her, enjoy her, she's your own: and let me be proud to tell you now, my lord, she's as good a soul, if a man had a mind to live honest and keep a wench, the kindest, sweetest, comfortablest rogue—

PRODITOR [Aside to **CAPTAIN**]
Hark in thine ear:
The baser slave art thou, and so I'll tell her;
I love the pearl thou sold'st, hate thee, the seller.
Go, to sea, the end of thee is lousy!

CAPTAIN
This is fine work! A very brave end, hum—

PRODITOR [Aside]
Well thought upon, this scrivener may furnish me.

[Takes **FIDELIO** aside.]

PHOENIX [Aside]
Why should this fellow be a lord by birth,
Being by blood a knave? One that would sell
His lordship if he lik'd her ladyship.

FIDELIO
Yes, my lord?

PHOENIX [Aside]
What's here, now?

PRODITOR
I have employment for a trusty fellow,
Bold, sure—

FIDELIO

What if he be a knave, my lord?

PRODITOR
There thou com'st to me; why he should be so,
And men of your quill are not unacquainted.

FIDELIO
Indeed, all our chief living, my lord, is by fools and knaves; we could not keep open shop else: fools that enter into bonds and knaves that bind 'em.

PRODITOR
Why, now we meet.

FIDELIO
And, as my memory happily leads me, I know a fellow of a standing estate, never flowing:
I durst convey treason into his bosom
And keep it safe nine years.

PRODITOR
A goodly time.

FIDELIO
And, if need were, would press to an attempt,
And cleave to desperate action.

PRODITOR
That last fits me.
Thou hast the measure right; look I hear from thee.

FIDELIO
With duteous speed.

PRODITOR
Expect a large reward.
I will find time of her to find regard.

[Exit.

FIDELIO [Aside to **PHOENIX**]
Oh, my lord,
I have strange words to tell you!

PHOENIX
Stranger yet?
I'll choose some other hour to listen to thee;
I am yet sick of this. Discover quickly.

FIDELIO [Aside to **PHOENIX**]

Why, will you make yourself known, my lord?

PHOENIX
Ay:
Who scourgeth sin, let him do't dreadfully.

CAPTAIN
Pox of his dissemblance! I will to sea.

PHOENIX [Aside]
Nay, you shall to sea, thou wouldst poison the whole land else. [To **CAPTAIN**] Why, how now, Captain?

CAPTAIN
In health.

FIDELIO
What, drooping?

PHOENIX
Or asham'd of the sale of thine own wife?

CAPTAIN
You might count me an ass, then, i'faith.

PHOENIX
If not asham'd of that, what can you be asham'd of, then?

CAPTAIN
Prithee ha' done; I am asham'd of nothing.

PHOENIX [Aside]
I easily believe that.

CAPTAIN
This lord sticks in my stomach.

PHOENIX
How? Take one of thy feathers down, and fetch, him up.

FIDELIO
I'd make him come.

PHOENIX
But what if the Duke should hear of this?

FIDELIO
Ay, or your son-in-law Fidelio know of the sale of his mother?

CAPTAIN

What and they did, I sell none but mine own. As for the DUKE, he's abroad by this time, and for Fidelio, he's in labour.

PHOENIX

He in labour?

CAPTAIN

What call you travelling?

PHOENIX

That's true. But let me tell you, Captain, whether the Duke hear on't, or Fidelio know on't, or both, or neither, 'twas a most filthy, loathsome part—

FIDELIO

A base, unnatural deed—

[They discover themselves, and lay hands on him.

CAPTAIN

Slave and fool! Ha, who? Oh!

PHOENIX

Thou hateful villain! Thou shouldst choose to sink
To keep thy baseness shrouded.

[Enter his lady **CASTIZA**.

FIDELIO

Ugly wretch!

CASTIZA

Who hath laid violence upon my husband,
My dear, sweet Captain? Help!

PHOENIX

Lady, you wrong your value;
Call you him dear that has sold you so cheap?

CASTIZA

I do beseech your pardon, good my lord.

[Kneels.]

PHOENIX

Rise.

FIDELIO

My abuse'd mother!

CASTIZA
My kind son,
Whose liking I neglected in this match.

FIDELIO
Not that alone, but your far happier fortunes.

CAPTAIN
Is this the scrivener and the farmer's son?
Fire on his lordship, he told me they travell'd.

PHOENIX
And see the sum told out to buy that jewel
More precious in a woman than her eye,
Her honour.
Nay, take it to you, lady, and I judge it
Too slight a recompense for your great wrong,
But that his riddance helps it.

CAPTAIN
'Sfoot, he undoes me!
I am a rogue and a beggar;
The Egyptian plague creeps over me already,
I begin to be lousy.

PHOENIX
Thus happily prevented, you're set free,
Or else made over to adultery.

CASTIZA
To heaven and to you my modest thanks.

PHOENIX
Monster, to sea! Spit thy abhorr'd foam
Where it may do least harm; there's air and room.
Thou'rt dangerous in a chamber, virulent venom
Unto a lady's name and her chaste breath.
If past this evening's verge the dukedom hold thee,
Thou art reserv'd for abject punishment.

CAPTAIN
I do beseech your good lordship, consider
The state of a poor, downcast Captain.

PHOENIX
Captain?

Off with that noble title, thou becom'st
It vilely; I ne'er saw the name fit worse:
I'll sooner allow a pander a Captain than thee.

CAPTAIN
More's the pity.

PHOENIX
Sue to thy lady for pardon.

CASTIZA
I give it without suit.

CAPTAIN
I do beseech your ladyship not so much for pardon as to bestow a few of those crowns upon a poor, unfeathered rover, that will as truly pray for you [Aside] and wish you hang'd—as any man breathing.

CASTIZA
I give it freely all.

PHOENIX
Nay, by your favour,
It will contain you, lady; [to **CAPTAIN**, giving him money] here, be gone!
Use slaves like slaves: wealth keeps their faults unknown.

CAPTAIN
Well, I'm yet glad, I've liberty and these;
The land has plagu'd me, and I'll plague the seas.

[Exit.

PHOENIX
The scene is clear'd, the bane of brightness fled;
Who sought the death of honour is struck dead.
Come, modest lady.

FIDELIO
My most honest mother!

PHOENIX
Thy virtue shall live safe from reach of shames;
That act ends nobly, preserves ladies' fames.

[Exeunt.

SCENE III – A Room in Falso's House

Enter Justice **FALSO, KNIGHT, JEWELLER'S WIFE**.

FALSO
Why, this is but the second time of your coming, kinsman; visit me oft'ner. Daughter, I charge you bring this gentleman along with you: gentleman. I cry ye mercy, sir, I call you gentleman still, I forget you're but a KNIGHT; you must pardon me, sir.

KNIGHT
For your worship's kindness; worship. I cry you mercy, sir, I call you worshipful still, I forget you're but a justice.

FALSO
I am no more, i'faith.

KNIGHT
You must pardon me, sir.

FALSO
'Tis quickly done, sir; you see I make bold with you, kinsman, thrust my daughter and you into one chamber.

KNIGHT
Best of all, sir. Kindred, you know, may lie anywhere.

FALSO
True, true, sir. Daughter, receive your blessing. [Aside to **JEWELLER'S WIFE**] Take heed the coach jopper not too much; have a care to the fruits of your body. [To **KNIGHT**] Look to her, kinsman.

KNIGHT
Fear it not, sir.

JEWELLER'S WIFE
Nay, father, though I say it, that should not say it, he looks to me more like a husband than a kinsman.

FALSO
I hear good commendations of you, sir.

KNIGHT
You hear the worst of me, I hope, sir. I salute my leave, sir.

FALSO
You're welcome all over your body, sir.

[Exeunt **KNIGHT** and **JEWELLER'S WIFE**.]

Nay, I can behave myself courtly, though I keep house i' th' country. What, does my Niece hide herself? Not present, ha? Latronello!

[Enter **LATRONELLO**.

LATRONELLO
Sir.

FALSO
Call my Niece to me.

LATRONELLO
Yes, sir.

[Exit.

FALSO
A foolish, coy, bashful thing it is; she's afraid to lie with her own uncle. I'd do her no harm, i'faith; I keep myself a widower o' purpose, yet the foolish girl will not look into't. She should have all, i'faith; she knows I have but a time, cannot hold long. See where she comes.

[Enter **NIECE**.

Pray, whom am I, Niece?

NIECE
I hope you're yourself,
Uncle to me and brother to my father.

FALSO
Oh, am I so? It does not appear so, for surely you would love your father's brother for your father's sake, your uncle for your own sake.

NIECE
I do so.

FALSO
Nay, you do nothing, Niece.

NIECE
In that love which becomes you best I love you.

FALSO
How should I know that love becomes me best?

NIECE
Because 'tis chaste and honourable.

FALSO
Honourable? It cannot become me, then, Niece,

For I'm scarce worshipful. Is this an age
To entertain bare love without the fruits?
When I receiv'd thee first, I look'd
Thou shouldst have been a wife unto my house,
And sav'd me from the charge of marriage.
Do you think your father's five thousand pound would ha' made me take you else? No, you should ne'er
ha' been a charge to me. As far as I can perceive yet by you, I've as much need to marry as e'er I had:
would not this be a great grief to your friends, think you, if they were alive again?

NIECE
'Twould be a grief indeed.

FALSO
Y'ave confess'd
All about house that young Fidelio,
Who in his travels does attend the prince,
Is your vow'd love.

NIECE
Most true, he's my vow'd husband.

FALSO
And what's a husband, is not a husband a stranger at first? And will you lie with a stranger before you lie
with your own uncle? Take heed what ye do, Niece, I counsel you for the best: strangers are drunken
fellows, I can tell you; they will come home late o' nights, beat their wives, and get nothing but girls!
Look to't, if you marry, your stubbornness is your dowry. Five thousand crowns were bequeathed to
you, true, if you marry with my consent; but if e'er you go to marrying by my consent, I'll go to hanging
by yours. Go to, be wise and love your uncle.

NIECE
I should have cause then to repent indeed.
Do you so far forget the offices
Of blushing modesty? Uncles are half father;
Why, they come so near our bloods they're e'en part of it.

FALSO
Why, now you come to me, Niece; if your uncle be part of your own flesh and blood, is it not then fit
your own flesh and blood should come nearest to you? Answer me to that, Niece.

NIECE
You do allude all to incestuous will,
Nothing to modest purpose. Turn me forth;
Be like an uncle of these latter days,
Perjur'd enough, enough unnatural;
Play your executorship in tyranny,
Restrain my fortunes, keep me poor, I care not.
In this alone most women I'll excel,
I'll rather yield to beggary than to hell.

[Exit.

FALSO
Very good! O' my troth, my Niece is valiant; she's made me richer by five thousand crowns, the price of her dowry. Are you so honest? I do not fear but I shall have the conscience to keep you poor enough, Niece, or else I am quite altered o' late.

[Enter **LATRONELLO**.

The news, may it please you, sir?

LATRONELLO
Sir, there's an old fellow, a kind of law-driver, entreats conference with your worship.

FALSO
A law-driver? Prithee, drive him hither.

[Exit **LATRONELLO**. Enter **TANGLE**.

TANGLE [To **SUITOR** offstage]
No, no, I say; if it be for defect of apparance, take me out a special significavit.

SUITOR [Within]
Very good, sir.

TANGLE
Then if he purchase an alias or capias, which are writs of custom, only to delay time, your procedendo does you knight's service, that's nothing at all; get your distringas out as soon as you can for a jury.

SUITOR [Within]
I'll attend your good worship's coming out.

TANGLE
Do, I prithee, attend me; I'll take it kindly, a voluntate.

FALSO
What, old Signior Tangle!

TANGLE
I am in debt to your worship's remembrance.

FALSO
My old master of fence: come, come, come, I have not exercis'd this twelve moons, I have almost forgot all my law-weapons.

TANGLE
They are under fine and recovery; your worship shall easily recover them.

FALSO
I hope so. [To **LATRONELLO**, within] When, there?

[Enter **LATRONELLO**.

LATRONELLO
Sir?

FALSO
The rapier and dagger foils, instantly.

[Exit **LATRONELLO**.

And what's thy suit to me, old Tangle? I'll grant it presently.

TANGLE
Nothing but this, sir, to set your worship's hand to the commendation of a knave whom nobody speaks well on.

FALSO
The more shame for 'em; what was his offence, I pray?

TANGLE
Vestras deducite culpas: nothing but robbing a vestry.

FALSO
What, what? Alas, poor knave! Give me the paper. He did but save the churchwardens a labour; come, come, he has done a better deed in't than the parish is aware of, to prevent the knaves; he robs but seldom, they once a quarter. Methinks 'twere a part of good justice to hang 'em at year's end, when they come out of their office, to the true terrifying of all collectors and sidemen.

TANGLE
Your worship would make a fruitful commonwealth's-man. The Constable lets 'em alone, looks on, and says nothing.

FALSO
Alas, good man, he lets 'em alone for quietness' sake, and takes half a share with 'em: they know well enough, too, he has an impediment in his tongue; he's always drunk when he should speak.

TANGLE
Indeed, your worship speaks true in that, sir: they blind him with beer and make him so narrow-eyed that he winces naturally at all their knaveries.

FALSO
So, so, here's my hand to his commendations.

[Signs the paper.

TANGLE
A caritate, you do a charitable deed in't, sir.

FALSO
Nay, if it be but a vestry matter, visit me at any time, old Signior Law-thistle!

[Enter **LATRONELLO** with rapier and dagger foils, and then exit.

Oh, well done, here are the foils; come, come, sir, I'll try a law-bout with you.

TANGLE
I am afraid I shall overthrow you, sir, i'faith.

FALSO
'Tis but for want of use, then, sir.

TANGLE
Indeed, that same odd word "use" makes a man a good lawyer, and a woman an arrant. Tuh, tuh, tuh, tuh, tuh! Now am I for you, sir; but first, to bring you into form, can your worship name all your weapons?

FALSO
That I can, I hope. Let me see, longsword, what's longsword? I am so dull'd with doing justice that I have forgot all, i'faith.

TANGLE
Your longsword, that's a writ of delay.

FALSO
Mass, that sword's long enough, indeed; I ha' known it reach the length of fifteen terms.

TANGLE
Fifteen terms? That's but a short sword.

FALSO
Methinks 'tis long enough; proceed, sir.

TANGLE
A writ of delay, longsword, scandala magnatum, backsword.

FALSO
Scandals are backswords, indeed.

TANGLE
Capias comminus, case of rapiers.

FALSO

Oh, desperate!

TANGLE
A latitat, sword and dagger. A writ of execution, rapier and dagger.

FALSO
Thou art come to our present weapon; but what call you sword and buckler, then?

TANGLE
Oh, that's out of use now! Sword and buckler was call'd a good conscience, but that weapon's left long ago; that was too manly a fight, too sound a weapon for these our days. 'Slid, we are scarce able to lift up a buckler now, our arms are so bound to the pox; one good bang upon a buckler would make most of our gentlemen fly i' pieces; 'tis not for these linty times. Our lawyers are good rapier and dagger men; they'll quickly dispatch your money.

FALSO
Indeed, since sword and buckler time, I have observ'd there has been nothing so much fighting; where be all our gallant swaggerers? There are no good frays o' late.

TANGLE
Oh, sir, the property's alter'd; you shall see less fighting every day than other, for every one gets him a mistress, and she gives him wounds enow; and, you know, the surgeons cannot be here and there, too: if there were red wounds too, what would become of the Rheinish wounds?

FALSO
Thou sayest true, i'faith; they would be but ill-favouredly look'd to then.

TANGLE
Very well, sir.

FALSO
I expect you, sir.

TANGLE
I lie in this court for you, sir; my rapier is my attorney, and my dagger his clerk.

FALSO
Your attorney wants a little oil, methinks; he looks very rustily.

TANGLE
'Tis but his proper colour, sir; his father was an iremonger. He will ne'er look brighter, the rust has so eat into him; h'as never any leisure to be made clean.

FALSO
Not in the vacation?

TANGLE
"Non vacat exiguis rebus adesse Jovi."

FALSO

Then Jove will not be at leisure to scour him, because he ne'er came to him before.

TANGLE

You're excellent at it, sir; and now you least think on't, I arrest you, sir.

FALSO

Very good, sir.

TANGLE

Nay, very bad, sir, by my faith; I follow you still, as the officers will follow you as long as you have a penny.

FALSO

You speak sentences, sir. By this time have I tried my friends, and now I thrust in bail.

TANGLE

This bail will not be taken, sir; they must be two citizens that are no cuckolds.

FALSO

By'rlady, then I'm like to lie by it; I had rather 'twere a hundred that were.

TANGLE

Take heed I bring you not an nisi prius, sir.

FALSO

I must ward myself as well as I may, sir.

TANGLE

'Tis court day now; declarat atturnatus, my attorney gapes for money.

FALSO

You shall have no advantage yet; I put in my answer.

TANGLE

I follow the suit still, sir.

FALSO

I like not this court, by'rlady. I take me out a writ of remove, a writ of remove, do you see, sir?

TANGLE

Very well, sir.

FALSO

And place my cause higher.

TANGLE

There you started me, sir; yet for all your demurs, pluries, sursurraras, which are all longswords, that's delays, all the comfort is, in nine years a man may overthrow you.

FALSO
You must thank your good friends then, sir.

TANGLE
Let nine years pass, five hundred crowns cast away o' both sides, and the suit not twenty; my counsellor's wife must have another hood, you know, and my attorney's wife will have a new forepart. Yet see at length law, I shall have law. Now beware, I bring you to a narrow exigent, and by no means can you avoid the proclamation.

[Knocks Falso's rapier from his hand.]

FALSO
Oh!

TANGLE
Now follows a writ of execution: a capias utlagatum gives you a wound mortal, trips up your heels, and lays you i' th' Counter.

[Overthrows him.]

TANGLE
I cry your worship heartily mercy, sir; I thought we had been in law together, adversarius contra adversarium, by my troth.

FALSO
Oh, reach me thy hand! I ne'er had such an overthrow in my life.

TANGLE
'Twas 'long of your attorney there; he might o' stayed the execution of capias utlagatum, and remov'd you with a supersedeas non molestandum into the court of equity.

FALSO
Pox on him, he fell out of my hand when I had most need of him.

TANGLE
I was bound to follow the suit, sir.

FALSO
Thou couldst do no less than overthrow me, I must needs say so.

TANGLE
You had recovered cost else, sir.

FALSO
And now, by th' mass, I think I shall hardly recover without cost.

TANGLE

Nay, that's certo scio; an execution is very chargeable.

FALSO

Well, it shall teach me wit as long as I am a justice. I perceive by this trial, if a man have a sound fall in law, he shall feel it in his bones all his life after.

TANGLE

Nay, that's recto upon record, for I myself was overthrown in eighty-eight by a tailor, and I have had a stitch in my side ever since. Oh!

[Exeunt.

ACT III

SCENE I – Falso's House

Toward the close of the music, the justice's three men prepare for a robbery, and exeunt. Enter Justice **FALSO**, untrussed.

FALSO

Why, Latronello, Furtivo, Fucato! Where be these lazy knaves that should truss me, not one stirring yet?

A CRY

Follow, follow, follow!

FALSO

What news, there?

A CRY

This way, this way! Follow, follow!

FALSO

Hark, you sluggish soporiferous villains! There's knaves abroad when you are a-bed: are ye not asham'd on't? A justice's men should be up first, and give example to all knaves.

[Enter two of his men; **LATRONELLO** and **FUCATO**, tumbling in, in false beards.

LATRONELLO

Oh, I beseech your good worship!

FUCATO

Your worshipful worship!

FALSO

Thieves! My two-hand sword! I'm robb'd i' th' hall! Latronello, knaves, come down; my two-hand sword, I say!

LATRONELLO
I am Latronello, I beseech your worship.

FALSO
Thou Latronello? Thou liest; my men scorn to have beards.

LATRONELLO
We forget our beards.

[They take off their false beards.

Now, I beseech your worship, quickly remember us.

FALSO
How now?

FUCATO
Nay, there's no time to talk of "how now"; 'tis done.

A CRY
Follow, follow, follow!

LATRONELLO
Four mark and a livery is not able to keep life and soul together: we must fly out once a quarter; 'tis for your worship's credit to have money in our purse. Our fellow Furtivo is taken in the action.

FALSO
A pox on him for a lazy knave! Would he be taken?

FUCATO
They bring him along to your worship; you're the next justice. Now or never show yourself a good master, an upright magistrate, and deliver him out of their hands.

FALSO
Nay, he shall find me apt enough to do him good, I warrant him.

LATRONELLO
He comes in a false beard, sir.

FALSO
'Sfoot, what should he do here else? There's no coming to me in a true one, if he had one. The slave to be taken! Do I not keep geldings swift enough?

LATRONELLO
The goodliest geldings of any gentleman in the shire.

FALSO
Which did the whoreson knave ride upon?

LATRONELLO
Upon one of your best, sir.

FUCATO
Stand-and-deliver.

FALSO
Upon Stand-and-deliver? The very gelding I choose for mine own riding; as nimble as Pegasus the flying horse yonder. Go, shift yourselves into your coats; bring hither a great chair and a little table.

FUCATO
With all present speed, sir.

FALSO
And Latronello—

LATRONELLO
Ay, sir?

FALSO
Sit you down, and very soberly take the examination.

LATRONELLO
I'll draw a few horse heads in a paper, make a show: I hope I shall keep my countenance.

[Exeunt **LATRONELLO** and **FUCATO**.

FALSO
Pox on him again! Would he be taken? He frets me. I have been a youth myself; I ha' seen the day I could have told money out of other men's purses—mass, so I can do now—nor will I keep that fellow about me that dares not bid a man stand: for as long as drunkenness is a vice, stand is a virtue. But I would not have 'em taken. I remember now betimes in a morning, I would have peep'd through the green boughs, and have had the party presently, and then to ride away finely in fear; 'twas e'en venery to me, i'faith, the pleasantest course of life! One would think every woodcock a **CONSTABLE**, and every owl an officer. But those days are past with me; and, o' my troth, I think I am a greater thief now, and in no danger. I can take my ease, sit in my chair, look in your faces now, and rob you; make you bring your money by authority, put off your hat, and thank me for robbing of you. Oh, there is nothing to a thief under covert bar'n!

[Enter **PHOENIX**, **FIDELIO** being robb'd; **CONSTABLE**, **OFFICERS** and the thief **FURTIVO**.

CONSTABLE
Come, officers, bring him away.

FALSO [Aside]
Nay, I see thee through thy false beard, thou mid-wind-chined rascal!—How now, my masters, what's he, ha?

CONSTABLE
Your worship knows I never come but I bring a thief with me.

FALSO
Thou hast left thy wont else, Constable.

PHOENIX
Sir, we understand you to be the only uprightness of this place.

FALSO
But I scarce understand you, sir.

PHOENIX
Why, then, you understand not yourself, sir.

FALSO
Such another word and you shall change places with the thief.

PHOENIX
A maintainer of equal causes, I mean.

FALSO
Now I have you; proceed, sir.

PHOENIX
This gentleman and myself, being led hither by occasion of business, have been offered the discourtesy of the country, set upon by three thieves, and robb'd.

FALSO
What are become of the other two? Latronello and Fucato!

PHOENIX
They both made away from us; the cry pursues 'em but as yet none but this taken.

[Enter **LATRONELLO** and **FUCATO**, with chair and table.

FALSO
Latronello.

LATRONELLO
Sir?

FALSO
Take his examination.

LATRONELLO

Yes, sir.

FALSO

Let the knave stand single.

FURTIVO

Thank your good worship.

FALSO

H'as been a suitor at court, sure; he thanks me for nothing.

PHOENIX

He's a thief now, sure.

FALSO

That we must know of him; what are you, sir?

FURTIVO

A piece next to the tail, sir: a serving-man.

FALSO

By my troth, a pretty phrase and very cleanly handled! Put it down, LATRONELLO; thou mayst make use on't. Is he of honour or worship whom thou servest?

FURTIVO

Of both, dear sir; honourable in mind and worshipful in body.

FALSO

Why, would one wish a man to speak better?

PHOENIX

Oh, sir, they most commonly speak best that do worst.

FALSO

Say you so, sir? Then we'll try him further. Does your right worshipful master go before you as an example of vice, and so encourage you to this slinking iniquity? He is not a lawyer, is he?

FURTIVO

H'as the more wrong, sir; both for his conscience and honesty, he deserves to be one.

FALSO

Pity he's a thief, i'faith; I should entertain him else.

PHOENIX

Ay, if he were not as he is, he would be better than himself.

FURTIVO
No, 'tis well known, sir, I have a master the very picture of wisdom—

LATRONELLO [Aside]
For indeed he speaks not one wise word.

FURTIVO
And no man but will admire to hear of his virtues—

LATRONELLO [Aside]
Because he ne'er had any in all his life.

FALSO
You write all down, Latronello?

LATRONELLO
I warrant you, sir.

FURTIVO
So sober, so discreet, so judicious—

FALSO
Hum.

FURTIVO
And above all, of most reverend gravity.

FALSO
I like him for one quality: he speaks well of his master; he will fare the better. Now, sir, let me touch you.

FURTIVO
Ay, sir.

FALSO
Why, serving a gentleman of such worship and wisdom, such sobriety and virtue, such discretion and judgment as your master is, do you take such a beastly course to stop horses, hinder gentlewomen from their meetings, and make citizens never ride but o' Sundays, only to avoid morning prayer and you? Is it because your worshipful master feeds you with lean spits, pays you with Irish money, or clothes you in northern dozens?

FURTIVO
Far be it from his mind, or my report. 'Tis well known he kept worshipful cheer the day of his wife's burial, pays our four marks a year as duly by twelve pence a quarter as can be—

PHOENIX [Aside]
His wisdom swallows it.

FURTIVO

And for northern dozens, fie, fie, we were ne'er troubled with so many.

FALSO
Receiving then such plenteous blessings from your virtuous and bountiful master, what cause have you to be thief now? Answer me to that gear.

FURTIVO
'Tis e'en as a man gives his mind to't, sir.

FALSO
How, sir?

FURTIVO
For alas, if the whole world were but of one trade, traffic were nothing; if we were all true men, we should be of no trade. What a pitiful world would here be! Heaven forbid we should be all true men: then how should your worship's next suit be made? not a tailor left in the land; of what stuff would you have it made? not a merchant left to deliver it; would your worship go in that suit still? You would ha' more thieves about you than those you have banish'd, and be glad to call the great ones home again to destroy the little.

PHOENIX
A notable rogue!

FALSO
O' my troth, a fine knave, and he's answered me gloriously. What wages wilt thou take after thou art hang'd?

FURTIVO
More than your worship's able to give; I would think foul scorn to be a justice then.

FALSO [Aside]
He says true, too, i'faith, for we are all full of corruption here.—Hark you, my friends.

PHOENIX
Sir?

FALSO
By my troth, if you were no crueller than I, I could find in my heart to let him go.

PHOENIX
Could you so, sir? The more pitiful justice you.

FALSO
Nay, I did but to try you; if you have no pity, I'll ha' none. Away, he's a thief, to prison with him!

FURTIVO
I am content, sir.

FALSO

Are you content? Bring him back; nay, then, you shall not go. I'll be as cruel as you can wish. You're content? Belike you have a trick to break prison, or a bribe for the officers.

CONSTABLE

For us, sir?

FALSO

For you, sir! What color's silver, I pray? You ne'er saw money in your life. I'll not trust you with him. Latronello and Fucato, lay hold upon him; to your charge I commit him.

FURTIVO

Oh, I beseech you, sir!

FALSO

Nay, If I must be cruel, I will be cruel.

FURTIVO

Good sir, let me rather go to prison.

FALSO

You desire that? I'll trust no prison with you; I'll make you lie in mine own house, or I'll know why I shall not.

FURTIVO

Merciful sir!

FALSO

Since you have no pity, I will be cruel.

PHOENIX

Very good, sir; you please us well.

FALSO

You shall appear tomorrow, sirs.

FURTIVO

Upon my knees, sir.

FALSO

You shall be hang'd out o' th' way. Away with him, Latronello and Fucato! Officers, I discharge you my house; I like not your company.
Report me as you see me, fire and fuel;
If men be Jews, justices must be cruel.

[Exeunt all but **PHOENIX** and **FIDELIO**].

PHOENIX

So, sir, extremes set off all actions thus;
Either too tame or else too tyrannous.
He being bent to fury, I doubt now
We shall not gain access unto your love,
Or she to us.

FIDELIO
Most wishfully, here she comes.

Enter NIECE.

PHOENIX
Is that she?

FIDELIO
This is she, my lord.

PHOENIX
A modest presence.

FIDELIO
Virtue bless you, lady.

NIECE
You wish me well, sir.

FIDELIO
I'd first encharge this kiss, and next this paper;
You'll know the language; 'tis Fidelio's.

NIECE
My ever-vowed love! How is his health?

FIDELIO
As fair as is his favour with the prince.

NIECE
I'm sick with joy: does the prince love him so?

FIDELIO
His life cannot requite it.
I had a token for you, kept it safe,
Till by misfortune of the way this morning
Thieves set upon this gentleman and myself,
And with the rest robb'd that.

NIECE
Oh, me, I'm dearly

Sorry for your chance! Was it your loss?
They boldly look you in the face that robb'd you;
No further villains than my uncle's men.

PHOENIX
What, lady?

NIECE
'Tis my grief I speak so true.

FIDELIO
Why, my lord!

PHOENIX
But give me pausing, lady; was he one
That took the examination?

NIECE
One, and the chief.

PHOENIX
Henceforth hang him that is no way a thief;
Then I hope few will suffer.
Nay, all the jest was, he committed him
To the charge of his fellows, and the rogue
Made it lamentable, cried to leave 'em.
None live so wise but fools may once deceive 'em!

FIDELIO
An uncle so insatiate!

PHOENIX
Ay, is't not strange, too,
That all should be by nature vicious,
And he bad against nature?

NIECE
Then you have heard the sum of all my wrongs?

PHOENIX
Lady, we have, and desire rather now
To heal 'em than to hear 'em.
For by a letter from Fidelio
Direct to us, we are entreated jointly
To hasten your remove from this foul den
Of theft and purpos'd incest.

NIECE

I rejoice
In his chaste care of me; I'll soon be furnish'd.

FIDELIO
He writes that his return cannot be long.

NIECE
I'm chiefly glad. But whither is the place?

PHOENIX
To the safe seat of his late wronged mother.

NIECE
I desire it.
Her conference will fit mine; well you prevail.

PHOENIX
At next grove we'll expect you.

NIECE
I'll not fail.

[Exeunt.

SCENE II – A Street

Enter **KNIGHT** and **JEWELLER'S WIFE**.

KNIGHT
It stands upon the frame of my reputation, I protest, lady.

JEWELLER'S WIFE
Lady: that word is worth an hundred angels at all times, for it cost more. If I live till tomorrow night, my sweet Pleasure, thou shalt have them.

KNIGHT
Could you not make 'em a hundred and fifty, think you?

JEWELLER'S WIFE
I'll do my best endeavour to multiply, I assure you.

KNIGHT
Could you not make 'em two hundred?

JEWELLER'S WIFE
No, by my faith—

KNIGHT
Peace, I'll rather be confin'd in the hundred and fifty.

JEWELLER'S WIFE
Come e'en much about this time, when taverns give up their ghosts, and gentlemen are in their first cast.

KNIGHT
I'll observe the season.

JEWELLER'S WIFE
And do but whirl the ring o' th' door once about; my maidservant shall be taught to understand the language.

KNIGHT
Enough, my sweet Revenue.

JEWELLER'S WIFE
Good rest, my effectual Pleasure.

[Exeunt.

ACT IV

SCENE I – A Street Before the Jeweller's House and the Court of Law]

Enter **PRODITOR** and **PHOENIX**.

PRODITOR
Come hither, Phoenix.

PHOENIX
What makes your honour break so early?

PRODITOR
A toy, I have a toy.

PHOENIX
A toy, my lord?

PRODITOR
Before thou layest thy wrath upon the DUKE,
Be advis'd.

PHOENIX

Ay, ay, I warrant you, my lord.

PRODITOR
Nay, give my words honour; hear me.
I'll strive to bring this act into such form
And credit amongst men, they shall suppose,
Nay, verily believe, the prince, his son,
To be the plotter of his father's murder.

PHOENIX
Oh, that were infinitely admirable!

PRODITOR
Were't not? It pleaseth me beyond my bliss.
Then if his son meet death as he returns,
Or by my hired instruments turn up,
The general voice will cry, "Oh, happy vengeance!"

PHOENIX
Oh, blessed vengeance!

PRODITOR
Ay, I'll turn my brain
Into a thousand uses, tire my inventions,
Make my blood sick with study, and mine eye
More hollow than my heart; but I will fashion,
Nay, I will fashion it. Canst counterfeit?

PHOENIX
The prince's hand? Most truly, most direct;
You shall admire it.

PRODITOR
Necessary mischief,
Next to a woman, but more close in secrets!
Thou'rt all the kindred that my breast vouchsafes.
Look into me anon: I must frame, and muse,
And fashion.

[Exit.

PHOENIX
'Twas to look into thee, in whose heart
Treason grows ripe, and therefore fit to fall;
That slave first sinks whose envy threatens all.
Now is his venom at full height.

FIRST VOICE WITHIN

"Lying or being in the said county, in the tenure and occupation aforesaid"—

SECOND VOICE WITHIN
No more, then; a writ of course upon the matter of—

THIRD VOICE WITHIN
Silence!

FOURTH VOICE WITHIN
Oho-o-o-yes! Carlo Turbulenzo, appear, or lose twenty mark in the suits.

PHOENIX
Ha? Whither have my thoughts conveyed me? I am now within the dizzy murmur of the law.

FIRST VOICE WITHIN
So that then, the cause being found clear, upon the last citation—

FOURTH VOICE WITHIN
Carlo Turbulenzo, come into the court.

[Enter **TANGLE** with **TWO SUITORS** after him.

TANGLE
Now, now, now, now, now, upon my knees I praise Mercury, the god of law! I have two suits at issue, two suits at issue.

FIRST SUITOR
Do you hear, sir?

TANGLE
I will not hear; I've other business.

FIRST SUITOR
I beseech you, my learned counsel—

TANGLE
Beseech not thee, beseech not me! I am a mortal man, a client as you are; beseech not me!

FIRST SUITOR
I would do all by your worship's direction.

TANGLE
Then hang thyself.

SECOND SUITOR
Shall I take out a special supplicavit?

TANGLE

Mad me not, torment me not, tear me not! You'll give me leave to hear mine own cause, mine own cause!

FIRST VOICE WITHIN
Nay, moreover, and further—

TANGLE
Well said, my lawyer, well said, well said!

FIRST VOICE WITHIN
All the opprobrious speeches that man could invent, all malicious invectives, called wittol to his face—

TANGLE
That's I, that's I; thank you, my learned counsel, for your good remembrance. I hope I shall overthrow him horse and foot.

FIRST SUITOR
Nay, but good sir—

TANGLE
No more, sir; he that brings me happy news first I'll relieve first.

BOTH SUITORS
Sound executions rot thy cause and thee!

[Exeunt **SUITORS**.

TANGLE
Ay, ay, pray so still, pray so still; they'll thrive the better.

PHOENIX
I wonder how this fellow keeps out madness?
What stuff his brains are made on?

TANGLE
I suffer, I suffer, till I hear a judgment!

PHOENIX
What, old signior?

TANGLE
Prithee, I will not know thee now; 'tis a busy time, a busy time with me.

PHOENIX
What, not me?

TANGLE

Oh, cry thee mercy! Give me thy hand; fare thee well. He's no relief again me, then; his demurs will not help him; his sursurraras will but play the knaves with him.

[Enter Justice **FALSO**.

PHOENIX
The justice, 'tis he.

FALSO
Have I found thee, i'faith? I thought where I should smell thee out, old Tangle.

TANGLE
What, old signior justicer? Embrace me another time, an you can possible. How does all thy wife's children? Well? That's well said, i'faith.

FALSO
Hear me, old Tangle.

TANGLE
Prithee, do not ravish me; let me go.

FALSO
I must use some of thy counsel first.

TANGLE
Sirrah, I ha' brought him to an exigent. Hark! That's my cause, that's my cause yonder! I twing'd him, I twing'd him!

FALSO
My Niece is stolen away.

TANGLE
Ah, get me a ne exeat regno quickly! Nay, you must not stay upon't, I'd fain have you gone.

FALSO
A ne exeat regno? I'll about it presently; adieu.

[Exit.

PHOENIX
You seek to catch her, justice; she'll catch you.

[Enter **FIRST SUITOR**.

FIRST SUITOR
A judgment, a judgment!

TANGLE

What, what, what?

FIRST SUITOR
Overthrown, overthrown, overthrown!

TANGLE
Ha? Ah, ah!

[Enter **SECOND SUITOR**.

SECOND SUITOR
News, news, news!

TANGLE
The devil, the devil, the devil!

SECOND SUITOR
Twice Tangle's overthrown, twice Tangle's overthrown!

TANGLE
Hold!

PHOENIX
Now, old cheater of the law—

TANGLE
Pray give me leave to be mad.

PHOENIX
Thou that hast found such sweet pleasure in the vexation of others—

TANGLE
May I not be mad in quiet?

PHOENIX
Very marrow, very manna to thee to be in law—

TANGLE
Very syrup of toads and preserv'd adders!

PHOENIX
Thou that hast vex'd and beggar'd the whole parish, and made the honest churchwardens go to law with the poor's money—

TANGLE
Hear me, do but hear me! I pronounce a terrible, horrible curse upon you all, and wish you to my attorney! See where a praemunire comes, a dedimus potestatem, and that most dreadful execution, excommunicato capiendo! There's no bail to be taken; I shall rot in fifteen jails: make dice of my bones,

and let my counsellor's son play away his father's money with 'em; may my bones revenge my quarrel! A capias comminus? Here, here, here, here; quickly dip your quills in my blood, off with my skin and write fourteen lines of a side. There's an honest, conscionable fellow; he takes but ten shillings of a bellows-mender. Here's another deals all with charity; you shall give him nothing, only his wife an embroidered petticoat, a gold fringe for her tail, or a border for her head. Ah, sirrah, you shall catch me no more in the springe of your knaveries!

[Exit.

FIRST SUITOR
Follow, follow him still; a little thing now sets him forward.

[Exeunt **SUITORS**.

PHOENIX
None can except against him; the man's mad,
And privileg'd by the moon, if he say true:
Less madness 'tis to speak sin than to do.
This wretch, that lov'd before his food his strife,
This punishment falls even with his life.
His pleasure was vexation, all his bliss
The torment of another;
Their hurt his health, their starved hopes his store:
Who so loves the law dies either mad or poor.

[Enter **FIDELIO**.

FIDELIO
A miracle, a miracle!

PHOENIX
How now, Fidelio?

FIDELIO
My lord, a miracle!

PHOENIX
What is't?

FIDELIO
I have found
One quiet, suffering, and unlawyer'd man;
An opposite, a very contrary
To the old turbulent fellow.

PHOENIX
Why, he's mad.

FIDELIO

Mad? Why, he is in his right wits: could he be madder than he was? If he be any way altered from what he was, 'tis for the better, my lord.

PHOENIX

Well, but where's this wonder?

FIDELIO

'Tis coming, my lord: a man so truly a man, so indifferently a creature; using the world in his right nature but to tread upon; one that would not bruise the cowardliest enemy to man, the worm, that dares not show his malice till we are dead. Nay, my lord, you will admire his temper! See where he comes.

[Enter **QUIETO**.

I promis'd your acquaintance, sir: yon is
The gentleman I did commend for temper.

QUIETO

Let me embrace you simply,
That's perfectly, and more in heart than hand;
Let affectation keep at court.

PHOENIX

Ay, let it.

QUIETO

'Tis told me you love quiet.

PHOENIX

Above wealth.

QUIETO

I above life; I have been wild and rash,
Committed many and unnatural crimes,
Which I have since repented.

PHOENIX

'Twas well spent.

QUIETO

I was mad, stark mad, nine years together.

PHOENIX

I pray, how?

QUIETO

Going to law, i'faith, it made me mad.

PHOENIX
With the like frenzy, not an hour since,
An aged man was struck.

QUIETO
Alas, I pity him!

PHOENIX
He's not worth pitying, for 'twas still his gladness
To be at variance.

QUIETO
Yet a man's worth pity;
My quiet blood has blest me with this gift:
I have cur'd some, and if his wits be not
Too deeply cut, I will assay to help 'em.

PHOENIX
Sufferance does teach you pity.

[Enter Quieto's **BOY**.

BOY
Oh, master, master! Your abominable next neighbour came into the house, being half in drink, and took away your best carpet.

QUIETO
Has he it?

BOY
Alas, sir!

QUIETO
Let him go; trouble him not. Lock the door quietly after him, and have a safer care who comes in next.

PHOENIX
But sir, might I advise you, in such a cause as this a man might boldly, nay, with conscience, go to law.

QUIETO
Oh, I'll give him the table too first! Better endure a fist than a sharp sword. I had rather they should pull off my clothes than flay off my skin and hang that on mine enemy's hedge.

PHOENIX
Why, for such good causes was the law ordain'd.

QUIETO
True, and in itself 'tis glorious and divine;
Law is the very masterpiece of heaven:

But see yonder,
There's many clouds between the sun and us,
There's too much cloth before we see the law.

PHOENIX
I'm content with that answer; be mild still:
'Tis honour to forgive those you could kill.

QUIETO
There do I keep.

PHOENIX
Reach me your hand; I love you,
And you shall know me better.

QUIETO
'Tis my suit.

PHOENIX
The night grows deep, and—

[Enter two **OFFICERS**.

FIRST OFFICER
Come away; this way, this way.

PHOENIX
Who be those? Stand close a little.

[As they retire, **PHOENIX** jars the ring of the Jeweller's door; the **MAID** enters, catches him.

MAID
Oh, you're come as well as e'er you came in your life; my master's new gone to bed. Give me your knightly hand: I must lead you into the blind parlour; my mistress will be down to you presently.

[Takes in **PHOENIX**, amazed.

FIRST OFFICER
I tell you, our safest course will be to arrest him when he comes out o' th' tavern, for then he will be half drunk and will not stand upon his weapon.

SECOND OFFICER
Our safest course indeed, for he will draw.

FIRST OFFICER
That he will, though he put it up again, which is more of his courtesy than of our deserving.

[Exeunt **OFFICERS**.

QUIETO
The world is nothing but vexation,
Spite, and uncharitable action.

FIDELIO
Did you see the gentleman?

QUIETO
Not I.

FIDELIO
Where should he be? It may be he's passed by;
Good sir, let's overtake him.

[Exeunt.

SCENE II – A Room in the Jeweller's House

Enter **PHOENIX** with the **MAID**.

MAID
Here, sir, now you are there, sir; she'll come to you instantly. I must not stay you; my mistress would be jealous. You must do nothing to me; my mistress would find it quickly.

[Exit.

PHOENIX
'Sfoot, whither am I led? Brought in by th' hand? I hope it can be no harm to stay for a woman, though indeed they were never more dangerous. I have ventured hitherto and safe, and I now must venture to stay now. This should be a fair room, but I see it not: the blind parlour calls it she?

[Enter **JEWELLER'S WIFE**.

JEWELLER'S WIFE
Where art thou, Oh, my Knight?

PHOENIX
Your Knight? I am the duke's Knight.

JEWELLER'S WIFE
I say you're my Knight, for I'm sure I paid for you.

PHOENIX
Paid for you? Hum; 'sfoot, a light!

[Snatches in a light, and then extinguishes it.

JEWELLER'S WIFE
Now out upon the marmoset! Hast thou serv'd me so long, and offer to bring in a candle?

PHOENIX [Aside]
Fair room, villainous face, and worse woman! I ha' learnt something by a glimpse o' th' candle.

JEWELLER'S WIFE
How happen'd it you came so soon? I look'd not for you these two hours. Yet, as the sweet chance is, you came as well as a thing could come, for my husband's newly brought abed.

PHOENIX
And what has Jove sent him?

JEWELLER'S WIFE
He ne'er sent him anything since I knew him: he's a man of a bad nature to his wife; none but his maids can thrive under him.

PHOENIX
Out upon him!

JEWELLER'S WIFE
Ay, judge whether I have a cause to be a courtesan or no? to do as I do? An elderly fellow as he is, if he were married to a young virgin, he were able to break her heart, though he could break nothing else. Here, here, there's just a hundred and fifty—

[Giving money]

—but I stole 'em so hardly from him, 'twould e'en have griev'd you to have seen it.

PHOENIX
So 'twould, i'faith.

JEWELLER'S WIFE.
Therefore, prithee, my sweet Pleasure, do not keep company so much. How do you think I am able to maintain you? Though I be a Jeweller's Wife, jewels are like women, they rise and fall; we must be content to lose sometimes to gain often: but you're content always to lose and never to gain. What need you ride with a footman before you?

PHOENIX
Oh, that's the grace!

JEWELLER'S WIFE
The grace? 'Tis sufficient grace that you've a horse to ride upon. You should think thus with yourself every time you go to bed: if my head were laid, what would become of that horse? He would run a bad race then, as well as his master.

PHOENIX
Nay, an you give me money to chide me—

JEWELLER'S WIFE
No, if it were as much more, I would think it foul scorn to chide you. I advise you to be thrifty, to take the time now while you have it; you shall seldom get such another fool as I am, I warrant you. Why, there's Matreza Auriola keeps her love with half the cost that I am at; her friend can go afoot like a good husband, walk in worsted stockings, and inquire for the sixpenny ordinary.

PHOENIX
Pox on't, and would you have me so base?

JEWELLER'S WIFE
No, I would not have you so base, neither: but now and then, when you keep your chamber, you might let your footman out for eightpence a-day; a great relief at year's end, I can tell you.

PHOENIX [Aside]
The age must needs be foul when vice reforms it.

JEWELLER'S WIFE
Nay, I've a greater quarrel to you yet.

PHOENIX
I'faith, what is't?

JEWELLER'S WIFE
You made me believe at first the prince had you in great estimation, and would not offer to travel without you, nay, that he could not travel without your direction and intelligence.

PHOENIX
I'm sorry I said so, i'faith, but sure I was overflown when I spoke it: I could ne'er ha' said it else.

JEWELLER'S WIFE
Nay, more: you swore to me that you were the first that taught him to ride a great horse, and tread the ring with agility.

PHOENIX
By my troth, I must needs confess I swore a great lie in that, and I was a villain to do it, for I could ne'er ride a great horse in my life.

JEWELLER'S WIFE
Why lo, who would love you now but a citizen's wife? So inconstant, so forsworn! You say women are false creatures, but take away men and they'd be honester than you. Nay, last of all, which offends me most of all, you told me you could countenance me at court, and you know we esteem a friend there more worth than a husband here.

PHOENIX
What I spake of that, lady, I'll maintain.

JEWELLER'S WIFE
You maintain? You seen at court?

PHOENIX
Why, by this diamond—

JEWELLER'S WIFE
Oh, take heed! you cannot have that; 'tis always in the eye of my husband.

PHOENIX
I protest I will not keep it, but only use it for this virtue: as a token to fetch you and approve my power, where you shall not only be received but made know to the best and chiefest.

JEWELLER'S WIFE
Oh, are you true?

PHOENIX
Le me lose my revenue else.

JEWELLER'S WIFE
That's you word indeed, and upon that condition take it, this kiss, and my love forever.

[Gives **PHOENIX** the diamond, and kisses him.]

PHOENIX
Enough!

JEWELLER'S WIFE
Give me thy hand; I'll lead thee forth.

PHOENIX [Aside]
I'm sick of all professions; my thoughts burn:
He travels best that knows when to return.

[Exeunt.

SCENE II – A Street Before the Jeweller's House

Enter **KNIGHT**, two **OFFICERS** after him.

KNIGHT
Adieu, farewell, to bed you, I to my sweet city-bird, my precious Revenue: the very thought of a hundred and fifty angels increases oil and spirit, ho!

FIRST OFFICER

I arrest you, sir.

KNIGHT
Oh!

FIRST OFFICER
You have made us wait a goodly time for you, have you not, think you? You are in your rouses and mulwines; a pox on you! And you have no care of poor officers staying for you.

KNIGHT
I drunk but one health, I protest, but I could void it now. At whose suit, I pray?

FIRST OFFICER
At the suit of him that makes suits, your tailor.

KNIGHT
Why, he made me the last; this, this that I wear.

FIRST OFFICER
Argo. Nay, we have been scholars, I can tell you; we could not have been knaves so soon else: for as in that notable city call'd London stand two most famous universities, Poultry and Woodstreet, where some are of twenty years' standing, and have took all their degrees from the Master's side down to the Mistress' side, the Hole, so in like manner—

KNIGHT
Come, come, come, I had quite forgot the hundred and fifty angels.

SECOND OFFICER
'Slid, where be they?

KNIGHT
I'll bring you to the sight of 'em presently.

FIRST OFFICER
A notable lad, and worthy to be arrested! We'll have but ten for waiting, and then thou shalt choose whether thou wilt run away from us, or we from thee.

KNIGHT
A match at running. Come, come, follow me!

SECOND OFFICER
Nay, fear not that.

KNIGHT
Peace; you may happen to see toys, but do not see 'em.

FIRST OFFICER
Pah!

KNIGHT
That's the door.

FIRST OFFICER
This?
Knocks.

KNIGHT
'Sfoot, officer, you have spilled all already!

FIRST OFFICER
Why?

KNIGHT
Why? You shall see; you should have but whirl'd the ring once about, and there's a maidservant brought up to understand it.

MAID [Opening the door]
Who's at door?

KNIGHT
All's well again. Phist, 'tis I, 'tis I.

MAID
You? What are you?

KNIGHT
Puh! Where's thy mistress?

MAID
What of her?

KNIGHT
Tell her one, she knows who, her Pleasure's here, say.

MAID
Her Pleasure? My mistress scorns to be without her pleasure at this time of night. Is she so void of friends, think you? Take that for thinking so!

[Gives him a box on the ear, and shuts the door.

FIRST OFFICER
The hundred and fifty angels are lock'd up in a box; we shall not see 'em tonight.

KNIGHT
How's this? Am I used like a hundred pound gentleman? Damn me if ever I be her pleasure again! Well, I must to prison.

FIRST OFFICER
Go prepare his room; there's no remedy. I'll bring him along; he's tame enough now.

[Exit **SECOND OFFICER**.

KNIGHT
Dare my tailor presume to use me in this sort?
He steals, and I must lie in prison for't.

FIRST OFFICER
Come, come, away, sir!

[Enter a **GENTLEMAN** with a **DRAWER**.

GENTLEMAN
Art sure thou sawest him arrested, drawer?

DRAWER
If mine eyes be sober.

GENTLEMAN
And that's a question. Mass, here he goes! He shall not go to prison; I have a trick shall bail him. Away!

[Exit **DRAWER**. The **GENTLEMAN** puts his hands over the **FIRST OFFICER'S** eyes, while the **KNIGHT** escapes.]

FIRST OFFICER
Oh!

GENTLEMAN
Guess, guess, who am I? Who am I?

FIRST OFFICER
Who the devil are you? Let go! A pox on you! Who are you? I have lost my prisoner.

GENTLEMAN
Prisoner? I've mistook; I cry you heartily mercy. I have done you infinite injury, o' my troth; I took you to be an honest man.

FIRST OFFICER
Where were your eyes? Could you not see I was an officer? Stop, stop, stop, stop!

GENTLEMAN
Ha, ha, ha, ha!

[Exeunt.

ACT V

SCENE I – The Presence Chamber in the Duke of Ferrara's Palace

Enter **PRODITOR** and **PHOENIX**.

PRODITOR
Now, Phoenix.

PHOENIX
Now, my lord.

PRODITOR
Let princely blood
Nourish our hopes; we bring confusion now.

PHOENIX
A terrible sudden blow.

PRODITOR
Ay; what day
Is this hangs over us?

PHOENIX
By th' mass, Monday.

PRODITOR
As I could wish; my purpose will thrive best.
'Twas first my birthday, now my fortune's day.
I see whom fate will raise needs never pray.

PHOENIX
Never.

PRODITOR
How is the air?

PHOENIX
Oh, full of trouble!

PRODITOR
Does not the sky look piteously black?

PHOENIX
As if 'twere hung with rich men's consciences.

PRODITOR

Ah, stuck not a comet like a curbuncle
Upon the dreadful brow of twelve last night?

PHOENIX

Twelve? No, 'twas about one.

PRODITOR

About one? Most proper,
For that's the Duke.

PHOENIX [Aside]

Well shifted from thyself.

PRODITOR

I could have wished it between one and two,
His son and him.

PHOENIX

I'll give you comfort, then.

PRODITOR

Prithee.

PHOENIX

There was a villainous raven seen last night
Over the presence chamber in hard justle
With a young eaglet.

PRODITOR

A raven? That was I; what did the raven?

PHOENIX

Marry, my lord, the raven. To say truth,
I left the combat doubtful.

PRODITOR

So 'tis still,
For all is doubt till the deed crown the will.
Now bless thy loins with freedom, wealth, and honour;
Think all thy seed young lords, and by this act
Make a foot-cloth'd posterity; now imagine
Thou see'st thy daughters with their trains borne up,
Whom else despised want may curse to whoredom,
And public shames, which our state never threat:
She's never lewd that is accounted great.

PHOENIX [Aside]

I'll alter that court-axiom, thus renew'd:
She's never great that is accounted lewd.

[Enter several **NOBLES**.

PRODITOR
Stand close; the presence fills. Here, here the place;
And at his rising let his fall be base,
Beneath thy foot.

PHOENIX
How for his guard, my lord?

PRODITOR
My gold and fear keep with the chief of them.

PHOENIX
That's rarely well.

[Hides behind the presence chair.]

PRODITOR [Aside]
Bold, heedless slave, that dares attempt a deed
Which shall in pieces rend him!—

[Enter **LUSSURIOSO** and **INFESTO**.

My lords both!

LUSSURIOSO
The happiness of the day!

PHOENIX [Aside]
Time my returning;
Treasons have still the worst, yet still are spurning.

[Enter the **DUKE** attended.

PRODITOR
The Duke!

PHOENIX [Aside]
I ne'er was gladder to behold him.

ALL
Long live your grace!

DUKE

I do not like that strain:
You know my age affords not to live long.

PRODITOR [Aside]
Spoke truer than you think for.

DUKE
Bestow that wish upon the prince our son.

PHOENIX [Aside]
Nay, he's not to live long, neither.

PRODITOR
Him as the wealthy treasure of our hopes,
You as possession of our present comfort,
Both in one heart we reverence in one.

PHOENIX [Aside]
Oh, treason of a good complexion!

[Horn winded. Enter **FIDELIO**.

DUKE
How now, what fresher news fills the court's ear?

PRODITOR
FIDELIO!

FIDELIO
Glad tidings to your grace!
The prince is safe return'd, and in your court—

DUKE
Our joy breaks at our eyes; the prince is come!

PRODITOR
Soul-quicking news! [Aside] Pale vengeance to my blood!

FIDELIO
By me presenting to your serious view
A brief of all his travels.

[Delivers a paper.]

DUKE
'Tis most welcome;
It shall be dear and precious to our eye.

PRODITOR [Aside to **PHOENIX**]
He reads; I'm glad he reads.
Now, take thy opportunity, leave that place.

PHOENIX
At his first rising let his fall be base.

PRODITOR
That must be altered now.

PHOENIX
Which, his rising or his fall?

PRODITOR
Art thou dull now?
Thou hear'st the prince is come.

DUKE
What's here?

PRODITOR
My lord?

DUKE [Reads]
"I have got such a large portion of knowledge, most worthy father, by the benefit of my travel"—

PRODITOR
And so he has, no doubt, my lord.

DUKE [Reads]
"That I am bold now to warn you of Lord Proditor's insolent treason, who has irreligiously seduc'd a
fellow and closely convey'd him e'en in the presence chair to murder you."

PHOENIX [Steps out and drops his dagger.]
Oh, guilty, guilty!

DUKE
What was that fell? What's he?

PHOENIX
I am the man.

PRODITOR [Aside]
Oh, slave!

PHOENIX
I have no power to strike.

PRODITOR [Aside]
I'm gone, I'm gone!

DUKE
Let me admire heaven's wisdom in my son.

PHOENIX
I confess it; he hir'd me—

PRODITOR
This is a slave:
'Tis forg'd against mine honour and my life;
For in what part of reason can 't appear,
The prince, being travell'd, should know treasons here?
Plain counterfeit—

DUKE
Dost thou make false our son?

PRODITOR
I know the prince will not affirm it.

FIDELIO
He can
And will, my lord.

PHOENIX
Most just, he may.

DUKE
A guard.

LUSSURIOSO
We cannot but in loyal zeal ourselves
Lay hands on such a villain.

[**ATTENDANTS** secure **PRODITOR**.

DUKE
Stay you; I find you here, too.

LUSSURIOSO
Us, my lord?

DUKE [Reads]
"Against Lussurioso and Infesto, who not only most riotously consume their houses in vicious gaming, mortgaging their livings to the merchant, whereby he with his heirs enter upon their lands; from whence this abuse comes, that in short time the son of the merchant has more lordships than the son of the

nobleman, which else was never born to inheritance: but that which is more impious, they most adulterously train out young ladies to midnight banquets, to the utter defamation of their own honours and ridiculous abuse of their husbands."

LUSSURIOSO
How could the prince hear that?

PHOENIX
Most true, my lord:
My conscience is a witness 'gainst itself;
For to that execution of chaste honour
I was both hir'd and led.

LUSSURIOSO
I hope the prince, out of his piteous wisdom,
Will not give wrong to us; as for this fellow,
He's poor, and cares not to be desperate.

[Enter Justice **FALSO**.

FALSO
Justice, my lord! I have my Niece stol'n from me;
She's left her dowry with me, but she's gone;
I'd rather have had her love than her money, I.
This, this is one of them. Justice, my lord!
I know him by his face; this is the thief.

PRODITOR
Your grace may now to milder sense perceive
The wrong done to us by this impudent wretch,
Who has his hand fix'd at the throat of law,
And therefore durst be desperate of his life.

DUKE
Peace! You're too foul; your crime is in excess:
One spot of him makes not your ulcers less.

PRODITOR
Oh!

DUKE [To **PHOENIX**]
Did your violence force away his Niece?

PHOENIX
No, my good lord, I'll still confess what's truth:
I did remove her from her many wrongs,
Which she was pleas'd to leave, they were so vile.

DUKE [To **FALSO**]
What are you nam'd?

FALSO
Falso, my lord, Justice Falso;
I'm known by that name.

DUKE
Falso, you came fitly;
You are the very next that follows here.

FALSO
I hope so, my lord; my name is in all the records, I can assure your good grace.

[Enter **NIECE** and **CASTIZA** behind.]

DUKE [Reads]
"Against Justice Falso"—

FALSO
Ah!

DUKE [Reads]
"Who, having had the honest charge of his Niece committed to his trust by the last will and testament of her deceased father, and with her all the power of his wealth, not only against faith and conscience detains her dowry, but against nature and humanity assays to abuse her body."

NIECE [Coming forward]
I'm present to affirm it, my lov'd lord.

FALSO
How? What make I here?

NIECE
Either I must agree
To loathed lust or despis'd beggary.

DUKE [To **FALSO**]
Are you the plaintiff here?

FALSO
Ay, my good lord,
For fault of a better.

DUKE
Seldom comes a worse.
[Reads] "And moreover, not contain'd in this vice only, which is odious too much, but against the sacred use of justice, maintains three thieves to his men"—

FALSO
Cuds me!

DUKE [Reads]
"Who only take purses in their master's liberty, where if any one chance to be taken, he appears before him in a false beard, and one of his own fellows takes his examination"—

FALSO [Aside]
By my troth, as true as can be, but he shall not know on't.

DUKE [Reads]
"And in the end will execute justice so cruelly upon him, that he will not trust him in a prison, but commit him to his fellows' chamber."

FALSO [Aside]
Can a man do nothing i' the country but 'tis told at court? There's some busy informing knave abroad, o' my life.

PHOENIX
That this is true, and these, and more, my lord,
Be it, under pardon, spoken for mine own;
He the disease of justice, these of honour
And this of loyalty and reverance:
The unswept venom of the palace.

PRODITOR
Slave!

PHOENIX
Behold the prince to approve it!

[Discovers himself.

PRODITOR
Oh, where?

PHOENIX
Your eyes keep with your actions; both look wrong.

PRODITOR
An infernal to my spirit!

ALL
My lord, the prince!

PRODITOR
Tread me to dust, thou in whom wonder keeps!

Behold, the serpent on his belly creeps.

PHOENIX
Rankle not my foot; away!
Treason, we laugh at thy vain-labouring stings;
Above the foot thou hast no power o'er kings.

DUKE
I cannot with sufficient joy receive thee,
And yet my joy's too much.

PHOENIX
My royal father,
To whose unnatural murder I was hir'd,
I thought it a more natural course of travel,
And answering future expectation,
To leave far countries and inquire mine own.

DUKE
To thee let reverence all her powers engage,
That art in youth a miracle to age.
State is but blindness; thou hadst piercing art:
We only saw the knee, but thou the heart.
To thee then power and dukedom we resign;
He's fit to reign whose knowledge can refine.

PHOENIX
Forbid it my obedience!

DUKE
Our word's not vain;
I know thee wise, canst both obey and reign.
The rest of life we dedicate to heaven.

ALL
A happy and safe reign to our new Duke!

PHOENIX
Without your prayers safer and happier!
Fidelio.

FIDELIO
My royal lord.

PHOENIX
Here, take this diamond:
You know the virtue on't; it can fetch vice.
Madam Castiza—

FIDELIO
She attends, my lord.

[Exit.

PHOENIX
Place a guard near us. [To **CASTIZA**] Know you yon fellow, lady?

CASTIZA [Coming forward]
My honour's evil!

PRODITOR
Torment again!

PHOENIX
So ugly are thy crimes,
Thine eye cannot endure 'em.
And that thy face may stand perpetually
Turn'd so from ours, and thy abhorred self
Neither to threaten wrack of state or credit,
An everlasting banishment seize on thee!

PRODITOR
Oh, fiend!

PHOENIX
Thy life is such it is too bad to end.

PRODITOR
May thy rule, life, and all that's in thee glad,
Have as short time as thy begetting had!

PHOENIX
Away! thy curse is idle.

[Exit **PRODITOR**.

The rest are under reformation,
And therefore under pardon.

ALL
Our duties shall turn edge upon our crimes.

FALSO [Aside]
'Slid, I was afraid of nothing but that for my thievery and bawdery I should have been turn'd to an innkeeper.

[Enter **JEWELLER'S WIFE** with **FIDELIO**.

My daughter! I am asham'd her worship should see me.

JEWELLER'S WIFE
Who would not love a friend at court? What fine galleries and rooms am I brought through! I had thought my Knight have shown his face here, I.

PHOENIX
Now, mother of pride and daughter of lust,
Which is your friend now?

JEWELLER'S WIFE
Ah, me!

PHOENIX
I'm sure you are not so unprovided to be without a friend here: you'll pay enough for him first.

JEWELLER'S WIFE
This is the worst room that ever I came in!

PHOENIX
I am your servant, mistress; know you not me?

JEWELLER'S WIFE
Your worship is too great for me to know: I'm but a small-timbered woman when I'm out of my apparel, and dare not venture upon greatness.

PHOENIX
Do you deny me then? Know you this purse?

JEWELLER'S WIFE
That purse? Oh, death, has the Knight serv'd me so?
Given away my favours?

PHOENIX
Stand forth!
Thou one of those for whose close lusts
The plague never leaves the city.
Thou worse than common: private, subtle harlot,
That dost deceive three with one feigned lip:
Thy husband, the world's eye, and the law's whip.
Thy zeal is hot, for 'tis to lust and fraud,
And dost not dread to make thy book thy bawd.
Thou'rt curse enough to husband's ill-got gains,
For whom the court rejects, his gold maintains.
How dear and rare was freedom wont to be!
Now few but are by their wives' copies free,

And brought to such a head that now we see
City and suburbs wear one livery.

JEWELLER'S WIFE
'Tis 'long of those, an't like your grace, that come in upon us, and will never leave marrying of our widows till they make 'em all as free as their first husbands.

PHOENIX
I perceive you can shift a point well.

JEWELLER'S WIFE
Let me have pardon, I beseech your grace, and I'll peach 'em all, all the close women that are; and upon my knowledge there's above five thousand within the walls and the liberties.

PHOENIX
A band! They shall be sent against the Turk:
Infidels against infidels.

JEWELLER'S WIFE
I will hereafter live so modestly
I will not lie with mine own husband, nor
Come near a man in the way of honesty.

FALSO [Kneeling]
I'll be her warrant, my lord.

PHOENIX
You are deceived;
You think you're still a justice.

FALSO
'Sfoot, worse than I was before I kneel'd! I am no justice now; I know I shall be some innkeeper at last.

JEWELLER'S WIFE
My father, 'tis mine own father!

PHOENIX
I should have wonder'd else, lust being so like.

NIECE
Her birth was kin to mine; she may prove modest:
For my sake, I beseech you, pardon her.

PHOENIX
For thy sake, I'll do more: Fidelio, hand her.
My favours on you both; next, all that wealth
Which was committed to that perjur'd's trust.

FALSO
I'm a beggar now; worse than an innkeeper!

[Enter **TANGLE**, mad.

TANGLE
Your mittimus shall not serve: I'll set myself free with a deliberandum, with a deliberandum, mark you!

DUKE
What's he? A guard!

PHOENIX
Under your sufferance,
Worthy father, his harm is to himself;
One that has lov'd vexation so much,
He cannot now be rid on't:
He's been so long in suits that he's law-mad.

TANGLE
A judgment, I crave a judgment, yea! Nunc pro tunc, corruptione alicujus. I peep'd me a raven in the face, and I thought it had been my solicitor: oh, the pens prick me!

[Enter **QUIETO**.

PHOENIX
And here comes he, wonder for temperance,
Will take the cure upon him.

QUIETO
A blessing to this fair assembly.

TANGLE
Away! I'll have none on't; give me an audita querela, or a testificandum, or a dispatch in twelve terms: there's a blessing, there's a blessing!

PHOENIX
You see th' unbounded rage of his disease.

QUIETO
'Tis the foul fiend, my lord, has got within him.
The rest are fair to this, this breeds in ink,
And to that colour turns the blood possess'd:
For instance, now your grace shall see him dress'd.

TANGLE
Ah hah! I rejoice then he's puzzled, and muzzled too:
Is't come to a cepi corpus?

QUIETO
Ah, good sir,
This is for want of patience.

TANGLE
That's a fool:
She never saw the dogs and the bears fight;
A country thing!

QUIETO
This is for lack of grace.

TANGLE
I've other business, not so much idle time.

QUIETO
You never say your prayers.

TANGLE
I'm advis'd by my learned counsel.

QUIETO
The power of my charm come o'er thee,
Place by degrees thy wits before thee;
With silken patience here I bind thee,
Not to move till I unwind thee.

TANGLE
Yea! Is my cause so muddy? Do I stick, do I stick fast?
Advocate, here's my hand; pull, art made of flint?
Wilt not help out? Alas, there's nothing in't!

PHOENIX
Oh, do you sluice the vein now?

QUIETO
Yes, my honour'd lord.

PHOENIX
Pray, let me see the issue.

QUIETO
I therefore seek to keep it.

[Opens **TANGLE'S** vein over a basin.

Now burst out,
Thou filthy stream of trouble, spite, and doubt!

TANGLE

Oh, an extent, a proclamation, a summons, a recognisance, a tachment, and injunction! A writ, a seizure, a writ of 'praisement, an absolution, a quietus est.

QUIETO

You're quieter, I hope, by so much dregs.
Behold, my lord.

PHOENIX

This! Why, it outfrowns ink.

QUIETO

'Tis the disease's nature, the fiend's drink.

TANGLE

Oh, sick, sick, Signior Plyfee, sick!
Lend me thy nightcap. Oh!

QUIETO

The balsam of a temperate brain
I pour into this thirsty vein,
And with this blessed oil of quiet,
Which is so cheap that few men buy it,
Thy stormy temples I allay:
Thou shalt give up the devil, and pray;
Forsake his works, they're foul and black,
And keep thee bare in purse and back.
No more shalt thou in paper quarrel,
To dress up apes in good apparel.
He throws his stock and all his flock
Into a swallowing gulf
That sends his goose unto his fox,
His lamb unto his wolf.
Keep thy increase,
And live at peace,
For war's not equal to this battle:
That eats but men, this men and cattle;
Therefore no more this combat choose,
Where he that wins does always lose,
And those that gain all, with this curse receive it,
From fools they get it, to their sons they leave it.

TANGLE

Hail, sacred patience! I begin to feel
I have a conscience now; truth in my words,
Compassion in my heart, and, above all,
In my blood peace's music. Use me how you can,

You shall find me an honest, quiet man.
Oh, pardon, that I dare behold that face!
Now I've least law I hope I have most grace.

PHOENIX
We both admire the workman and his piece.
Thus, when all hearts are tun'd to honour's strings,
There is no music to the quire of kings.

[Exeunt **OMNES**.

Thomas Middleton – A Short Biography

Thomas Middleton was born in London in April 1580 and baptised on 18th April. He was the son of a bricklayer who had raised himself to the status of a gentleman and become the owner of property adjoining the Curtain Theatre in Shoreditch.

Middleton was aged only five when his father died. His mother remarried but this new union unfortunately fell apart and turned into a fifteen year legal conflict centered on the inheritance of Thomas and his younger sister.

Middleton went on to attend Queen's College, Oxford, matriculating in 1598. However he failed to graduate for reasons unknown leaving either in 1600 or 1601. He had by that time written and published three long poems in popular Elizabethan styles. None appears to have been commercially successful although Microcynicon: Six Snarling Satirese was denounced by the Archbishop of Canterbury and publicly burned as part of his attack on verse satire. Although a minor work, the poems show the roots of Middleton's interest in, and later mature work on, sin, hypocrisy, and lust.

In the early years of the 17th century, Middleton made a living writing topical pamphlets, including one, Penniless Parliament of Threadbare Poets, that was reprinted several times as well as becoming the subject of a parliamentary inquiry.

For one so young he was already making quite an impact and had obviously attracted the eye of the authorities in those turbulent times.

Records surviving of the great theatrical entrepreneur of the day, Philip Henslowe, confirm that Middleton was writing for Henslowe's Admiral's Men. His lauded contemporary, a certain William Shakespeare, was writing only for Henslowe whereas Middleton remained a free agent and able to write for whichever theatrical company hired him.

These early years writing plays continued to attract controversy. His friendship and writing partnership with Thomas Dekker brought him into conflict with Ben Jonson and George Chapman in the so-called War of the Theatres. (This controversy was also called the Poetomachia by Thomas Dekker. The Bishops Ban of 1599 had removed any use of satire from prose and verse publications and so the only outlet was on the stage. For the next 3 years Ben Jonson and George Chapman on one side and John Marston, Thomas Dekker and Thomas Middleton on the other poked fun at their opposition with characters from their plays. The grudge against Jonson continued as late as 1626, when Jonson's play The Staple of News indulges in a slur on Middleton's last play, A Game at Chess).

In 1603, Middleton married. It was also a momentous year in other respects. On the death of Elizabeth I, her cousin James VI of Scotland was now also crowned King James I of England. Another outbreak of the plague now forced the theatres in London to close.

For Middleton the changeover from Elizabethan to Jacobean was the beginning of a long period of success as a writer.

When the theatres re-opened and welcomed back audiences in need of entertainment Middleton was there, writing for several different companies. In particular he specialised in city comedy and revenge tragedy.

During this time he appears also to have written with Shakespeare and he is variously attributed as collaborating on All's Well That Ends Well and Timon of Athens.

Although Middleton had started as a junior partner to Thomas Dekker he was now his fully fledged equal. His finest work with Dekker was undoubtedly The Roaring Girl, a biography of the notorious contemporary thief Mary Frith (Frith began her criminal career as a pickpocket before moving on to highway robbery with a penchant for dressing up as a man. A spell in prison was followed by a long career as a 'fence' from her shop in Fleet St. She lived to the then quite extraordinary age of 74.) The writing is noteworthy not only for its playwriting ambition but in producing a fully formed heroine in Moll Cutpurse. This was only shortly after the role of women in plays had seen fit to have them played, in the main, by men.

In the 1610s, Middleton began another playwriting partnership, this time with the actor William Rowley, producing another slew of plays including the classics Wit at Several Weapons and A Fair Quarrel.

The ever adaptable Middleton seemed at ease working with others or by himself. His solo writing credits include the comic masterpiece, A Chaste Maid in Cheapside, in 1613. Interestingly his solo plays are somewhat less thrusting and bellicose. Certainly there is no comedy among them with the satirical depth of Michaelmas Term and no tragedy as raw, striking and as bloodthirsty as The Revenger's Tragedy.

There may be various reasons for this and among them that he was increasingly involved with civic pageants and therefore was trying to avoid too much controversy especially without the cover of a collaborator. Indeed in 1620, he was officially appointed as chronologer of the City of London, a post he held until his death in 1627, when ironically, it passed to his great rival, and sometime enemy, Ben Jonson.

Middleton's official duties did not interrupt his dramatic writing; the 1620s saw the production of his and Rowley's tragedy, and continual favourite, The Changeling, as well as several other tragicomedies.

However in 1624, he reached a peak of notoriety when his dramatic allegory A Game at Chess was staged by the King's Men. The play used the conceit of a chess game to present and satirise the recent intrigues surrounding the Spanish Match; James I's son, Prince Charles, was being positioned to marry the daughter, Maria Anna of the Spanish King Philip IV of Spain. Though Middleton's approach was strongly patriotic, the Privy Council closed the play, after only nine performances at the Globe theatre, having received a complaint from the Spanish ambassador. The Privy Council then opened a prosecution against both authors and actors. Although Middleton in his defence showed that the play had been passed by the Master of the Revels, Sir Henry Herbert, any further performance was forbidden and the author and actors fined.

What happened next is a mystery. It is the last play recorded as having being written by Middleton. His playwriting career appears to have stopped dead. It follows that some sort of further punishment probably occurred and for a writer can there be any greater punishment than not being allowed to write or be heard?

Middleton's work is diverse even by the standards of his age. His career Middleton covers many many genres including tragedy, history and city comedy. As we have noted he did not have the kind of official relationship with a particular company that Shakespeare or Fletcher had that might have supported him in a lean creative period. Instead he appears to have written on a freelance basis for any number of companies. His output ranges from the "snarling" satire of Michaelmas Term, performed by the Children of Paul's, to the bleak intrigues of The Revenger's Tragedy, performed by the King's Men. Interestingly earlier editions of The Revenger's Tragedy attributed the play solely to Cyril Tourneur but recent studies have shredded that view so that Middleton's authorship is not now seriously contested

Indeed modern techniques in analysing writing styles are now leaning towards giving Middleton credit for his adaptation and revision of Shakespeare's Macbeth and Measure for Measure. Along with the more established evidence of collaboration on All's Well That Ends Well and Timon of Athens it appears that Middleton has moved some way forward to the front rank of playwrights and an association, in some form, but its greatest exponent.

His early work was informed by the blossoming, in the late Elizabethan period, of satire, while his maturity was influenced by the ascendancy of Fletcherian tragicomedy. Middleton's later work, in which his satirical fury is tempered and broadened, includes three of his acknowledged masterpieces. A Chaste Maid in Cheapside, produced by the Lady Elizabeth's Men, which skillfully combines London life with an expansive view of the power of love to effect reconciliation even though London seems populated entirely by sinners, in which no social rank goes unsatirised. The Changeling, a later tragedy, returns Middleton to an Italianate setting like that of The Revenger's Tragedy, except that here the central characters are more fully drawn and more compelling as individuals. Similar development can be seen in Women Beware Women.

Middleton's plays are marked by their cynicism, though often very funny, about the human race. His characters are complex. True heroes are a rarity: almost all of his characters are selfish, greedy, and self-absorbed.

When Middleton does portray good people, the characters are often presented as flawless and perfect and given small, undemanding roles. A theological pamphlet attributed to Middleton gives sustenance to the notion that Middleton was a strong believer in Calvinism.

Thomas Middleton died at his home at Newington Butts in Southwark in the summer of 1627, and was buried on July 4th, in St Mary's churchyard which today survives as a public park in Elephant and Castle.

Middleton stands with John Fletcher and Ben Jonson as the most successful and prolific of playwrights from the Jacobean period. Very few Renaissance dramatists would achieve equal success in both comedy and tragedy but Middleton was one. He also wrote many masques and pageants and remains, to this day, one of the most notable of Jacobean dramatists.

Middleton's work has long been praised by many literary critics, among the most fervent were Algernon Charles Swinburne and T. S. Eliot. The latter thought Middleton was second only to Shakespeare.

Among their contemporaries was a very crowded field of talent including: Ben Jonson (1572-1637), Christopher Marlowe (1564-1593), Francis Beaumont (1585-1616), Henry Chettle (1564-1606), John Fletcher (1579–1625), John Ford (1586–1639), John Day (1574-1640), John Marston (1576-1634), John Webster (1580-1634), Nathan Field (1587-1620), Philip Massinger (1584-1640), Richard Burbage (1567-1619), Robert Greene (1558-1592), Thomas Dekker (1575-1625), Thomas Kyd (1558-1594), William Haughton (died 1605), William Rowley (1585-1626).

It's a daunting list and confirms that to top that made you a very special talent indeed.

Thomas Middleton – A Concise Bibliography

It has long been recognised that the modern concept of authorship was rather more elastic in centuries past. Writers were not only for hire, and their work therefore a commodity, but their plays ran much shorter lengths; two weeks being a common term of performance. To that themes and scenes were liberally excised from one play and used in another. Revisions to past plays that were being restaged would be undertaken and entirely credited to other writers. Many works and plays were unpublished and have not survived and some only from memory by actors etc. Whilst many of these playwrights are only now feted for their talents, some undoubtedly were at the time, but it is difficult to, in every case, to establish exact provenance. With modern scholarly and literary techniques author attributions have sometimes changed or been re-balanced. For those where this may be the case we have placed the *Play's Title and other information* in italics

Plays
Blurt, Master Constable or The Spaniard's Night Walk (with Thomas Dekker (1602)
The Phoenix (1603–4)
The Honest Whore, Part 1, a city comedy (1604), (with Thomas Dekker)
Michaelmas Term, a city comedy, (1604)
All's Well That Ends Well (1604-5); believed by some to be co-written by Middleton based on stylometric analysis.
A Trick to Catch the Old One, a city comedy (1605)
A Mad World, My Masters, a city comedy (1605)
A Yorkshire Tragedy, a one-act tragedy (1605); attributed to Shakespeare on its title page, but stylistic analysis favours Middleton.
Timon of Athens a tragedy (1605–6); stylistic analysis indicates that Middleton may have written this play in collaboration with William Shakespeare.
The Puritan (1606)
The Revenger's Tragedy (1606). Earlier editions often mistakenly attribute authorship to Cyril Tourneur.

Your Five Gallants, a city comedy (1607)
The Family of Love (1607) some attribute this to Middleton others include Dekker and Lording Barry.
The Bloody Banquet (1608–9); co-written with Thomas Dekker.
The Roaring Girl, a city comedy depicting the exploits of Mary Frith (1611); with Thomas Dekker.
No Wit, No Help Like a Woman's, a tragic-comedy (1611)
The Second Maiden's Tragedy, a tragedy (1611); an anonymous manuscript; stylistic analysis indicates Middleton's authorship (though one scholar also attributed it to Shakespeare.
A Chaste Maid in Cheapside, a city comedy (1613)
Wit at Several Weapons, a city comedy (1613); printed as part of the Beaumont and Fletcher Folio, but stylistic analysis indicates comprehensive revision by Middleton & Rowley.
More Dissemblers Besides Women, a tragicomedy (1614)
The Widow (1615–16)
The Witch, a tragicomedy (1616)
A Fair Quarrel, a tragicomedy (1616). Co-written with William Rowley.
The Old Law, a tragicomedy (1618–19). written with William Rowley and perhaps a third collaborator.
Hengist, King of Kent, or The Mayor of Quinborough, a tragedy (1620)
Women Beware Women, a tragedy (1621)
Measure for Measure (1603-4); some scholars argue that the First Folio text was partly revised by Middleton in 1621.
Anything for a Quiet Life, a city comedy (1621). Co-written with John Webster.
The Changeling, a tragedy (1622). Co-written with William Rowley.
The Nice Valour (1622). Printed as part of the Beaumont and Fletcher Folio, but stylistic analysis indicates comprehensive revision by Middleton.
The Spanish Gypsy, a tragicomedy (1623). Believed to be a play by Middleton & Rowley and later revised by Thomas Dekker and John Ford.
A Game at Chess, a political satire (1624). Satirized the negotiations over the proposed marriage of Prince Charles, son of James I of England, with the Spanish princess. Closed after nine performances.

Masques & Entertainments
The Whole Royal and Magnificent Entertainment Given to King James Through the City of London (1603–4). Co-written with Thomas Dekker, Stephen Harrison & Ben Jonson.
The Manner of his Lordship's Entertainment
The Triumphs of Truth
Civitas Amor
The Triumphs of Honour and Industry (1617)
The Masque of Heroes, or, The Inner Temple Masque (1619)
The Triumphs of Love and Antiquity (1619)
The World Tossed at Tennis (1620). Co-written with William Rowley.
Honourable Entertainments (1620–1)
An Invention (1622)
The Sun in Aries (1621)
The Triumphs of Honour and Virtue (1622)
The Triumphs of Integrity with The Triumphs of the Golden Fleece (1623)
The Triumphs of Health and Prosperity (1626)

Poetry

The Wisdom of Solomon Paraphrased (1597)
Microcynicon: Six Snarling Satires (1599)
The Ghost of Lucrece (1600)
Burbage epitaph (1619)
Bolles epitaph (1621)
Duchess of Malfi (commendatory poem) (1623)
St James (1623)
To the King (1624)

Prose
The Penniless Parliament of Threadbare Poets (1601)
News from Gravesend. Co-written with Thomas Dekker (1603)
The Nightingale and the Ant aka Father Hubbard's Tales (1604)
The Meeting of Gallants at an Ordinary (1604). Co-written with Thomas Dekker.
Plato's Cap Cast at the Year 1604 (1604)
The Black Book (1604)
Sir Robert Sherley his Entertainment in Cracovia (1609) (translation).
The Two Gates of Salvation (1609), or The Marriage of the Old and New Testament.
The Owl's Almanac (1618)
The Peacemaker (1618)

www.ingramcontent.com/pod-product-compliance
Lightning Source LLC
Chambersburg PA
CBHW060123050426
42448CB00010B/2012